DECORATING
CERAMICS

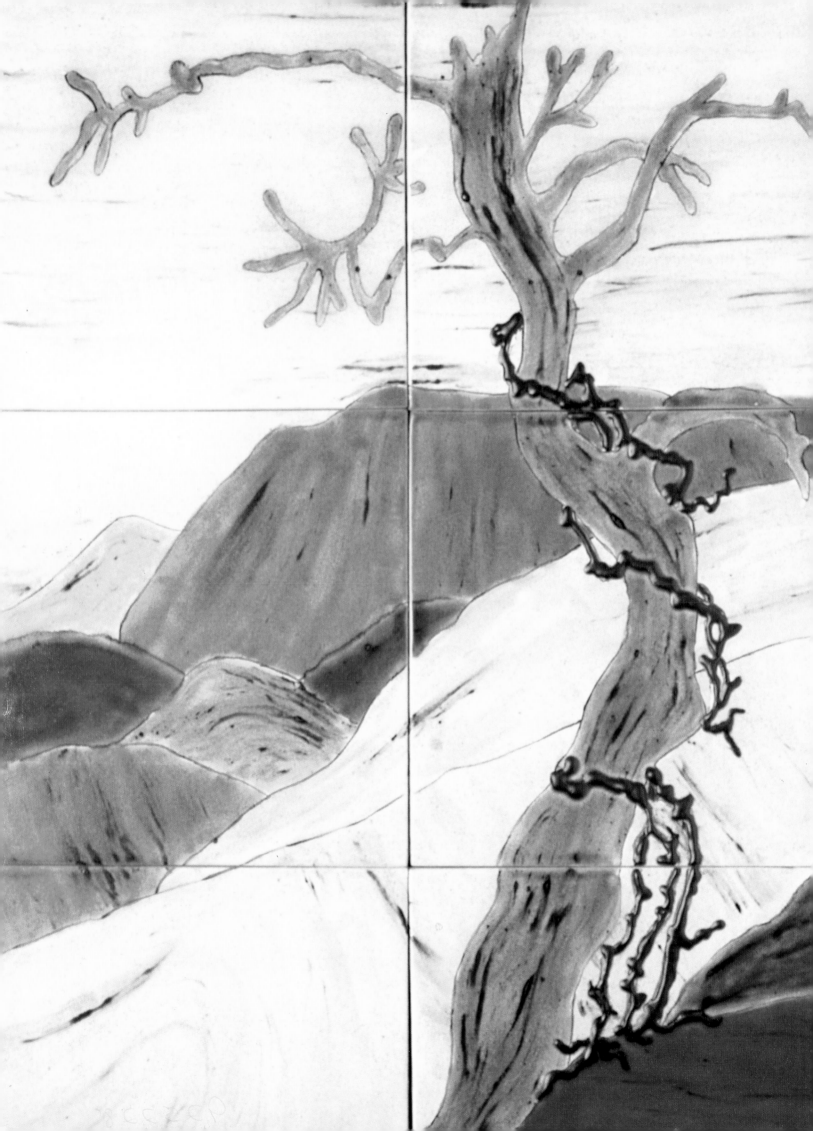

DECORATING CERAMICS

A GUIDE TO THE HISTORY,
MATERIALS, EQUIPMENT,
AND TECHNIQUES
OF ORNAMENTING CERAMIC
OBJECTS WITH APPLIED,
INCISED, AND PAINTED
DECORATION

M. Pilar Navarro

WATSON-GUPTILL PUBLICATIONS
NEW YORK

This edition first published in the United States in 1996 by Watson-Guptill
Publications, a division of BPI Communications, Inc., 1515 Broadway, New York,
New York 10036

First published in 1994 by Parramón Ediciones, S.A., Barcelona, Spain
©1994 Parramón Ediciones, S.A.

Editorial Director: Jordi Vigué
Assistant Editor: Jordi Martínez
Graphic Design: Josep Guasch i Cabanas
Photography: Nós & Soto
Illustrations: M. Pilar Navarro
Translation: Mark Lodge
Production: Rafael Marfil Mata

Library of Congress Cataloging-in-Publication Data

Navarro, M. Pilar.
[Decoración de cerámica.   English]
Decorating ceramics : a guide to the history, materials, equipment, and techniques of ornamenting ceramic objects with applied, incised, and painted decoration / M. Pilar Navarro.
          p.   cm.
ISBN 0-8230-3910-2 (pbk.)
1. Pottery craft. 2. Decoration and ornament. I. Title.
TT920.N38   1996
738.1'5–dc20   96-23970
                                               CIP

Manufactured in Spain

1 2 3 4 5 6 7 / 02 01 00 99 98 97 96

Contents

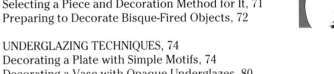

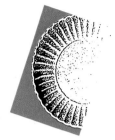

WHAT IS CERAMICS DECORATION?

The art of decorating ceramics is a combination of acquired technique and personal aesthetic expression. Painting and adornment usually begin after the shape and function of the piece have been determined. But the design of an object integrates both modeling and painting to such an extent that it's often difficult to distinguish where one ends and the other begins.

A piece may be decorated at any stage of the process. Your embellishment can be as simple as a subtle impression in the damp clay, as complex as a design painted on glazed ware, or myriad possibilities in between. All are forms of decoration.

The shape and texture of a piece often leads the ceramist to a particular type of adornment. Nonetheless, it is the artist's imagination and creativity that lends individuality and eye appeal to the shape, texture, and finish of each piece.

Before embarking on an experimental project, first you should familiarize yourself with basic procedures for obtaining the best results.

Reial Monestir de Sant Cugat del Valles

This book was written to inspire and instruct those who would like to develop skills in the fascinating craft of decorating ceramics. It will teach you all you need to know to begin creating your own handsome pieces.

But before you begin, I believe that knowing the general history of this genre will deepen your appreciation of any ceramic object that you see or contemplate designing. To supplement the historical review offered below, I recommend that you visit museums and study the great range of pottery created through the ages. Such knowledge will help you to identify the origin of particular pieces and act as valuable reference for ideas in designing your own work.

The second part of this book catalogues all the materials and equipment you'll need to carry out the various decorative techniques that are explained in the third section, where step-by-step instructions, fully illustrated, will guide you through each process. A handy glossary of terms follows that.

Of course, even the finest artists never attain one-hundred-percent originality in their work. But with experimentation, persistence, and creative self-expression, any dedicated artisan—even a novice—can bring a fresh "signature" to ceramic decoration.

Creating lovely functional and/or decorative ceramic pieces is a very gratifying experience. It is my hope that you will find in it as much pleasure as I have.

HISTORY

Although this volume is not intended to be a textbook on the history of ceramics, it does discuss the evolution of various techniques employed, from ancient times to the present—information that I believe will enhance your artistic expression. Part of the enjoyment of working in this medium is its rich heritage. Many of the techniques used today have been known for centuries. If you share with me a curiosity to learn new things—and the fact that you're reading this book indicates that you do—you'll be interested in finding out just where and when these techniques came about. I have selected the ones that I consider to be most important, giving brief comments and information for each.

People of the Paleolithic Age were nomadic hunters and food gatherers. Most experts agree that the prehistoric art that has survived from those millennia, stone carvings and painted and incised depictions of humans and animals on the walls of caves, were created to serve a magical function. During the later Stone Age, the Neolithic period, when nomadic peoples settled down, formed communities, began growing crops and domesticating animals, their art expression took on practical forms. They had to collect water, store grain and other foodstuffs, and discovered, almost certainly by chance, that by kneading clay and then cooking it over fire, they could produce vessels to serve such needs. It is presumed that women were the first potters, while men erected dolmens and other stone monoliths created for religious purposes. Those earliest potters might have adorned their vessels so that they could readily be differentiated from others and recognized by their respective owners. But the artistic impulse soon asserted itself, and the practice of decorating ceramics for purely aesthetic reasons was born.

The art of working clay quickly developed, and over the centuries, numerous techniques have been employed. But modern ceramists have a direct connection with all their predecessors, for even today, clay is still shaped primarily with the hands, just as it was thousands of years ago.

▲ Pre-Columbian earthenware cup. Decorated in a style typical of the period: short diagonal strokes incised in soft clay, formed into two encircling bands. Private collection.

► Earthenware pitcher. Simply painted, bold, spontaneous brushstrokes form a stylized floral design.

▼ Porcelain. The roses on this small tray were painted on top of a porcelain glaze, then fired again at a lower temperature. M. Pilar Navarro.

These three very obviously different styles illustrate just a sampling of the broad range of possibilities open to you in decorating ceramics.

Early Ceramics: Neolithic Chinese, Iberian, Pre-Columbian

Earliest Designs

Primitive ceramic decoration was based mainly on simple geometric motifs. When human or animal figures were incorporated, they often represented symbols of magic or worship to guard against evil spells. Similar figures also decorated many vessels that were not directly connected with the performance of rites. Pottery colors vary, depending on where the ceramic piece was produced, since the color is determined by the clay from which it was made. Because various types of clay can be found in the same region, it was quite common to use one kind as a decorative material to adorn another, such as black clay on white pottery or an ocher shade over red.

For primitive paints, bone ash was often used as white pigment, copper oxide for greens and blues, manganese compounds for black, antimony salts for yellows, and copper salts for red. They probably mixed some of these elements together or with certain clays to extend their color range.

Neolithic Chinese Pottery

While several styles of Chinese Neolithic pottery survive, one aspect of their decoration is fairly uniform: parallel grooves, triangles, and spirals. Red, black, orange, yellow, and pink are the dominant colors.

It was during the Shang dynasty (1766–1122 B.C.) that a light-green earthenware appeared whose composition included kaolin—a fine white clay that was much later associated with Ming porcelain. Art scholars have classified this ceramic as protoporcelain because they believe that not only does its whiteness and translucency qualify it as porcelain, but also because the hard and vitrified material produces a resonant, metallic sound when struck.

The importance given to funerals in early cultures dictated the kinds of the ceramics that were often produced. Amphorae—large jugs with handles—were filled with wine, and, together with vessels for all sorts of foods, were placed in a tomb so that the deceased would not feel lonely, thereby preventing the dead from returning to haunt their relatives. Thanks to the influence of Confucianism, a tradition of also placing in the tomb living pets, slaves, and concubines was finally abandoned after the sixth century B.C.

The discovery in 1974 of the tomb of Shih Hwang-ti, the first Chinese emperor, unearthed one of the greatest ceramics finds of all time. The tomb was built at the same time as the Great Wall and was actually an enormous underground palace that contained a huge army of life-size, perfectly proportioned and very realistic terra-cotta soldiers buried to protect the emperor. Many of the figures still retained their multicolored embellishments.

This monumental excavation is still in progress, but it has been estimated that inside this tomb, the figures total ten thousand men, five hundred horses, and over a hundred war chariots, all carrying weapons and found arranged in perfect military procession—every figure, animal, and chariot made to full scale, life size.

The Han dynasty of this period was a rich, happy time of plenty. Palaces, fountains, and towers were produced with opulent, minute details of adornment. In pottery, some clay figures were surfaced with green lead enamel to simulate bronze.

▲ **Iberian.** This bowl from circa third century B.C. is decorated with running hunters, foliage, and swag pattern.

▼ **Chinese.** Sketches of Tang Dynasty (A.D. 618–907) funereal statuettes; pottery of this type was either covered or flecked with glaze or left its clay color.

▶ **Neolithic Chinese.** Urn, 3000–1750 B.C. The Metropolitan Museum of Art, New York.

▲ **Pre-Columbian**. The vessel on this barking dog's back is for burning incense. A Mexican piece, it dates from the tenth to twelfth centuries B.C.

Japanese Pottery

The earliest pottery found in excavations in Japan date to 5000 B.C. and are regarded as being superior to all other pottery of the same Neolithic period. Either incisions or simple additions of clay adornment were used.

The later Jomon style (2000–900 B.C.) stands out for its painstaking decorations of superimposed clay piping coiled to form arabesques. A thick, granular type of clay, the rich substance from the earth used by these ancient artisans symbolized their love of anything that reflected nature, a fundamental characteristic of all Japanese art. Among the Jomon pieces, many splendid fertility idols have been identified.

Ceramics from the Yayoi culture (250 B.C.–A.D. 250) were particularly impressive for their simple, but concise, more realistic shapes. Vessels were made using the wheel; bottles had long, narrow necks; cooking pots were flat; and decorations featured fine incisions and the use of bright red paint. The great Haniwa figures (A.D. 400–552) of red terra-cotta have a very simple structure—*Haniwa* means clay cylinder—and were placed outside and around important tombs.

Mesopotamian School

Noteworthy early pottery from this region is adorned with animals or geometric stylizations. Similar to Mesopotamian, in Persia, Nihavand and Susa styles were employed. In Susa, walls were decorated with colored glazed tiles.

Ancient painted decorations have been located in Mesopotamia in the fertile plain between the Tigris and the Euphrates, where communication and trade joined Asia, Africa, and Europe. Owing to continual invasions and emigrations, homogeneous populations were not easily consolidated, resulting in increased intermixing of artistic styles. The Sumerians were the first to settle and introduce Mesopotamian culture. After many invasions and wars, Babylon was founded and eventually became the capital of a great empire that stretched as far as the Persian Gulf. It was later conquered by the Persians, whose power grew to such an extent that they were a threat to Greece and the rest of the Mediterranean peoples.

The cultural wealth of the Mesopotamian civilization is known to us in many ways, starting with King Hammurabi's famous Code of Laws. In architecture, innovations included the first arch construction, and the use of clay bricks fired by the sun's rays, as a substitute for stone construction, because the region had no quarries. Soon pottery production began. Then the ceramist would fashion clay into desired shapes, submerge them in a bath of diluted, colored clay, fire the pieces slowly in an open kiln, having first decorated them with incisions made before firing.

▲ **Mesopotamian school.** Vase found in a necropolis in Iran.

▲ **Neolithic Japanese.** Vase of the Jomon period.

◄ **Neolithic Japanese.** Sketch showing a popular style of the period, Jomon, which means coiled rope, considered the most sophisticated of ceramics produced at that time.

◄ **Mesopotamian.** Glazed tiles depicting the archers of Darius I, king of Persia, from his palace wall at Susa.

11

Egyptian and Pre-Hellenic Pottery

◀ **Egyptian pottery.** Fragment of an eighteenth-dynasty enameled vase decorated with a border of manganese brushstrokes.

into the clay, then the piece is baked in a single firing, producing a glassy coating, often turquoise in color. Distinctive surface motifs in Egyptian ceramics often derive from native flora, the lotus and papyrus being most characteristic.

Pre-Hellenic Pottery

B eginning in about 2500 B.C., Minoan and Helladic styles of pre-Hellenic pottery were characteristically red in color and decorated with marine motifs such as octopuses, seaweed, and seashells.

Extremely elegant pots, later made on the wheel, often had a bright black coating with a violet sheen, freely decorated in a style that tends toward naturalism. Some have dark backgrounds, others are light or even white, and still others are reddish. The pieces have thin walls, decorated with slip that forms embossed patterns.

The technique demanded precision work, and large teams of people were involved in the production and sale of this pre-Hellenic pottery.

▲ **Pre-Hellenic pottery.** This seventh-century-B.C. pot with stylized animal figure atop its lid has a lively pattern that mixes a band of running circular design with a vertical zigzag pattern. Kestner museum, Hanover, Germany.

▼ **Pre-Hellenic pottery.** Dating from about 2000 B.C., this Minoan vessel, with its bold, freely rendered contemporary-looking pattern, could easily be mistaken for a piece created in our own twentieth century.

Egyptian Pottery

T he great civilization of ancient Egypt owed its prosperity to the fertility of the Nile valley and the genius of its people. Such wonders as the pyramids and the Great Sphinx at Gizeh were built, which still command the world's awe thousands of years later. Not only in architecture did ancient Egypt distinguish itself during the span of thirty pharaonic dynasties. Great discoveries were made in medicine, astronomy, and hydraulics, and Egyptian artistry produced brilliant work in ivory, bronze, textiles, glass, furniture, jewelry, and, of course, ceramics.

The art of pottery came to Egypt via Mesopotamia; the first examples were clay covered in black or red slip with sgraffito (Italian for scratched) incisions filled with a whitish clay, whose designs ranged from the geometric to depictions of sailing boats and human figures.

But many believe that the greatest achievement of Egyptian pottery was the invention of one of the earliest glazes, still known today as Egyptian paste. While most glazes are applied on top of clay, this substance is mixed

Etruscans inhabited the Italian peninsula from about 800 B.C. or earlier. Some examples of their pottery with rudimentary decorations have also been found in Sardinia, Sicily, and Switzerland.

Essentially, the earliest Etruscan pottery was a crude imitation of previous Greek styles, particularly in the rendering of certain figures and geometrics.

One highly original product should be mentioned: the black, wheel-made pitcher. The clay used was dark, fine-grained, and rich in iron, which gave a shiny, metallic-looking surface when rubbed with resin or wax and then burnished with a piece of hard wood.

Strangely enough, pre-Columbian pottery blackened by firing was also given the name *búcaro* (pitcher) shortly after it was discovered, but today this term is used only for Etruscan pottery.

► **Etruscan pottery.** This goblet with handles was created in the middle of the sixth century B.C.

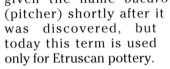

► **Etruscan pottery.** An amphora from Attica, with black figures that show Achilles killing Penthesilea, dates to 525 B.C. British Museum, London.

◄ **Etruscan pottery.** A fifth-century-B.C. jug with vertical groove pattern has an extended pouring spout.

13

Greek Pottery

◄ **Greek pottery.** Krater, for mixing wine and water, decorated in the highly accomplished red-figure painting style.

Greek pottery stands out in history for the timeless beauty of its shapes and graceful embellishments. The clays used varied considerably, depending on their region of origin. In the east, from Rhodes and the Aegean Islands, it was reddish and granular; on the Greek mainland, in Attica and Laconia, it was lighter in shade and had a smoother, more refined consistency; but to the south in Corinth, the clay was quite yellow.

Large quantities of oil and wine had to be shipped as well as stored, thus, easily transportable containers were needed. Vessels made of clay satisfied both requirements. Pottery for these and other commodities were designed and named for their particular functions. The best known, the amphora, had an oval body, narrow mouth and neck with handles on either side. The base was pointed so that deliveries of amphorae could be anchored in the sand when they were unloaded on beaches. In addition to holding liquids, amphorae were also used for the storage of pickled foods. Other useful vessels were the lekythos, a long-handled, cylindrical jug for oils and funereal ointments; the kylix, a shallow drinking goblet with two handles; the pyxis, a covered dressing-table box; the hydria, a three-handled water jar; and the oenochoe, a jug with a trefoil-shaped mouth for pouring wine.

The wheel that was used to make these pieces was rudimentary, consisting of a plate supported by a vertical axis that was turned by the potter or an assistant. During the drying stage, the potter checked the shape and, if necessary, corrected any imperfections, using a bone or a piece of wood.

Oriental influence, plus inspiration drawn from Mesopotamia and Egypt, always governed the decoration of Rhodes pottery. Designs featured a black area on a light-colored slip, within which geometric figures were drawn.

Greek pottery production flourished in Athens. The quality of its red clay, rich in iron oxide, together with superb designs and craftsmanship, made the city the center of pottery production. Black-figure painting on red clay was sometimes heightened by the use of a light-colored slip to depict flesh. Figures and garments were often rendered in minute detail.

There are two great names associated with the technique of black-figure painting. The Amasis Painter (his real name is unknown) was an excellent sixth-century-B.C. miniaturist who specialized in decorating pots; attributed to him are more than one hundred pieces, depicting human figures, lotus flowers, palm trees, and other flora. During the same period, Exekias, considered by some to have been the finest artist of his time, is known by only eleven signed works of boldly drawn, almost relief-outlined figures.

In a continuing quest for artistic excellence, the technique of red-figure vase painting was developed late in the sixth century B.C. A background of black was created from glaze, leaving the figures in the natural color of the red clay. Remarkably fine details, painted with thin black lines, were then added within the figures, which often depicted heroic narrative themes.

This laborious technique was gradually perfected over the years. There are three well-defined historical periods: the severe style, the classical, and the mannerist.

▼ **Greek pottery.** Third-century-B.C. Etruscan vase.

► **Greek pottery.** Detail of a vase created by the Amasis Painter.

Roman Pottery

When Rome expanded and formed an empire, the life and customs of its inhabitants changed, and their interest in objects for domestic and ornamental purposes grew.

Great quantities of patterned dishes were produced in factories in which the workers were often slaves from Asian lands. Often they marked the bottom of the pottery to identify the worker's origin. The clay used was obtained by decanting and it was of a very fine grain, quite compact, with a lot of iron and a little calcium. The piece was bathed in a clay slip that ensured a smooth surface; the reddish shade partly depended on where the clay was from and on the oxidizing atmosphere during firing.

Pieces were also made from molds that perfectly reproduced highly complex reliefs.

With the expansion of the empire through Alexandria into Egypt, the Romans acquired the glazing techniques long practiced there, using a base of lead colored with iron, copper, or manganese oxide.

▲ **Roman pottery.** Examples of many styles of vases, urns, and pots with incised and other adornments.

◄ **Roman pottery.** Examples of trays, jug, and bowls.

▲ Byzantine pottery. These plate fragments show three techniques: incisions, marbling, and glaze-coated relief.

▼ Pre-Columbian pottery. From Peru, a double bottle with a bridging handle with a design that includes seven corncobs, one of which has anthropomorphic characteristics. Ethnological Museum, Barcelona.

Byzantine Pottery

Not much is known about Byzantine pottery because of the small numbers of pieces that have survived. The great siege that Constantinople suffered at the hands of the Turks in the fifteenth century considerably reduced production and absorbed the Islamic prototype.

By studying fragments that have been found, some features of Byzantine pottery can be established. During the Byzantine Empire (395–1453), the iron-bearing red clay and lead-bearing glaze methods that had been learned from Egypt and Rome were commonly employed. Pots were fashioned on the wheel, and the ovens in use produced a good firing quality. In addition to household pottery, ornamental mosaics and wall tiles were made, thereby bringing the art of ceramics to architecture. Byzantines worked with sgraffito, the technique of scratching through one layer of slip to reveal another color beneath. After crosshatching the slip overlay with stylized fantasy depictions, the artist would cover the piece with a greenish transparent glaze mixed with black or brown. An extremely attractive effect was achieved by then coating the piece with a thin film of multicolored slip that produced marblelike veins; the slip was then covered with a colorless, or slightly yellow, lead glaze. Other techniques such as relief work were used to mark the piece with the factory stamp. Decoration was varied and clearly religious in nature. It absorbed influences from Oriental cultures, and in its turn, aspects of Byzantine work inspired Western art.

Pre-Columbian Ceramics

When using the term pre-Columbian, we refer to art made by the indigenous peoples of the Americas before Christopher Columbus's first voyage in 1492. Major centers of ceramic development were in Central America, South America, and areas of southwestern United States.

Since the wheel was unknown, clay was shaped by hand, and coiling construction was usually employed—clay rolled into thin strips then coiled into pots. Shapes varied depending on where the pieces were made, but in general, they were round or oval and thin-walled. The clays used were of a wide variety of colors, and slip adornment was often added.

Many pre-Columbian pots were decorated or shaped in animal or human forms. Plants and geometric patterns are also found, and unornamented pottery was not uncommon. Given the vast expanse of territory involved, such a wide variety of artistic expression is quite natural. Of the

▼ Pre-Columbian pottery. This Mayan pot has a stylized narrative depiction.

◀ **Pre-Columbian ceramics.** This anthropomorphic figure traces to the Tairona, one of the most advanced cultures in Colombia. From the Caribbean coast, valley of the Magdalena River. Private collection.

▼ **Pre-Columbian pottery.** Rudimentary clay bowls belonging to the Simú culture. Only one of them has some faint incisions on the rim. Private collection.

many pre-Columbian cultures, the most well known are the Inca, Aztec, and Maya, but other tribes of the Americas made important contributions to ceramic production.

The Chibcha people, or Muisca, of central Colombia, created a narrow-necked, oval-shaped vessel with long, flat handles that is still made by potters in the region today, as it was in pre-Columbian times. The Tairona, an extinct tribe from northern Colombia, used an iron-based glaze that gave pots a shiny black finish. The most ancient pre-Columbian pieces have been found in that region, dating from the year 3000 B.C.

In China, during the Shang dynasty (1766–1122 B.C.), a yellow or brownish glaze was used that was fired at a high temperature. We could say that the glaze is comparable to a crystal that has melted over the surface of the clay. There are not too many elements that can form crystals; the most easily found and most plentiful is silica. So the potters added dissolvents as well as alumina to make the dissolvents and silica adhere better to the clay.

One of the most ancient methods of glazing consisted of coating the unfired clay with copper or lead powder and then firing it.

Glazes not only add significantly to the beauty of ceramic pieces. A glaze makes pottery more impermeable, improves its solidity, and makes it easier to clean.

Earliest Glazes

Among the most ancient glazed pieces known to us are those created by the Assyrians. Celadon glaze—the distinctive gray-green finish that originated in China—dates back to 1300 B.C. But it is believed, though not yet proved, that the first glazing took place in the Nile valley some two thousand years earlier.

What has been verified, however, is that luster and enamels were being applied to crafts by Egyptian artisans in about 2700 B.C., during the third dynasty, which tells us that they probably did know about glazing.

▶ **Early glazed pot.** A grayish-pink glaze covers this pot of unknown origin.

Lusterware

uster is an iridescent metallic decoration applied to glazed ceramic wares, which are then fired again at low temperatures, giving a bright sheen. This ancient technique was probably devised by Syrian and Egyptian artisans. The pigments used contained silver, copper, and sulfur oxides, which produced the iridescent luster.

Islamic Lusterware

ollowing the seventh-century-A.D. territorial conquests made by the Arabs in the name of Mohammed, much magnificent Islamic pottery was produced over the next thousand years. Its quality was so fine that some scholars deem it the best the world has ever created.

While it was the glazers of Egypt and Syria who first tried luster painting, the technique was developed in Baghdad and Samarra (in Iraq), then eventually extended to Mesopotamia and into Persia.

During its long and glorious history, from the seventh to the seventeenth century, Islamic pottery underwent many changes, incorporating a variety of techniques and styles. Craftspeople of the time moved freely from country to country and enriched their knowledge by learning new techniques that they adapted to their own work. Such influences are also reflected in painting, architecture, and illuminated books and documents.

Early Islamic human and animal designs were quite static, though they nevertheless had boldness and impact. But it wasn't until the twelfth century that figural paintings on ceramics became endowed with greater movement and delicacy. Quotes and proverbs from the Koran were often incorporated in graceful calligraphy embossed into the wet clay or superimposed by adding material to create bas-relief effects.

Continued discoveries were made, most notably, that cobalt and manganese pigments remained stable under an alkaline glaze. A more practical and economical technique, it replaced previous ones.

Unfortunately, much of the wealth of pottery that existed was destroyed by Mongol invasions of the area. Only the Persian city of Kashan, in the middle of the twelfth century, was able to revive the luster tradition, although mainly for painting tiles decorated with intricate geometric designs for the walls and floors of mosques and tombs.

The Islamic style had a considerable influence on Spanish and Italian pottery and spread to such an extent that it reached as far as India.

▲ **Islamic lusterware.** A twelfth-century plate honoring a religious authority shown with liturgical symbols, painted in a single color and delicately pierced with a graver.

▼ **Islamic lusterware.** A molded lusterware Persian vase from the twelfth century combines a repeat pattern of a human figure with an arabesque and foliate pattern.

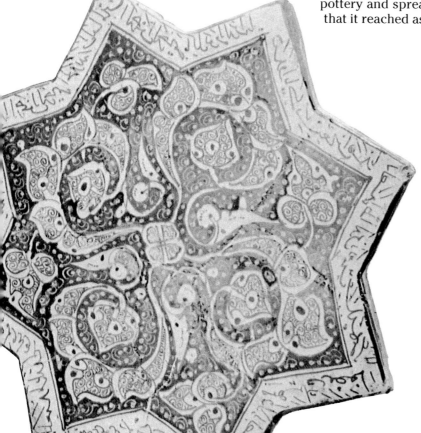

◄ **Islamic lusterware.** This eight-pointed-star floor tile, decorated with bold arabesques of a single color, has a border of calligraphic design.

Lusterware from the Iberian Peninsula

Although the Moorish invasion of the Iberian Peninsula brought suffering to the populace, it also marked the beginning of great educational and cultural development in that part of the world.

In 756, the Umayyad prince Abd ar-Rahman I proclaimed himself emir of Córdoba and set in motion the establishment of a thriving cultural center where sciences and the arts, including pottery making, flourished. Córdoba became the capital of Moslem Spain, where there still stands the Great Mosque, built in stages between 786 and 987.

Under the Caliphate of Córdoba, other extraordinary Moorish architecture was erected, some of it no longer standing. But excavations have unearthed among its ruins examples of very high-quality pottery, including some with early tin glazes. Interestingly, many lusterware fragments show that the pieces were not made with local clays.

As the Umayyad dynasty ended, pottery making went into decline. What remained became scattered, but records indicate active twelfth-century pottery production centers in Almería, Murcia, and particularly in Málaga.

Islamic artisans excelled in palace architecture, and no more beautiful example exists than the Alhambra in Granada, residence of the last Moslem rulers of Spain. Magnificent remains include lustrous tiles and intricately adorned vases probably made by Málaga potters, whose work has been found on sites as far apart as England and Egypt. When Castilian kings came to power in 1487, production of top-quality Málaga pottery came to an end.

As power shifted in many parts of Spain, an inevitable period of political and economic upheaval ensued, forcing ceramists and other artisans to relocate as they searched for locales of greater stability. Among those who settled in the kingdom of Valencia were the accomplished ceramists

▲ **Iberian lusterware.** An enameled brazier of the majolica type, circa 1430. The Metropolitan Museum of Art, New York.

▲ **Iberian lusterware.** On this monochrome sixteenth-century plate, an ornately dressed female figure is surrounded by arabesque designs.

Joan Albalat and Pascassi Martí, who were commissioned to make floor tiles for the palace of the cardinal of Avignon. Another craftsman famous for his decorating was Jehan from Valencia, known as the Saracen, who did work for the Duke of Berry.

By the end of the fifteenth century, lusterware and the Islamic style began to lose favor. It was supplanted by Renaissance art, which was heavily patronized by Spanish monarchs. Newfound Western influences in art showed particular preference for the Italian school, which dominated tastes of the period.

▼ **Iberian lusterware.** The coat of arms of a monastery abbot is set against a stylized foliate background on this sixteenth-century vase painted in two colors with metallic highlights.

Italian Lusterware of the Renaissance

Although some Moslem influence had spilled over into the boot of Italy from Sicily during the few centuries when that island embraced Islam, interest in lusterware did not appear on the mainland until the sixteenth century.

It is not known with certainty if Spanish potters traveled to Italy and introduced their techniques there, or if it was the Italians who went to the Iberian Peninsula to learn them. But we do know that considerable interchange and trade in various commodities took place between the two nations. Florence, for example, established banks and warehouses in Barcelona to speed up commercial transactions. Majorca served as a port of linkage between Spain and Italy; the word majolica comes from that island's name. At first the term referred only to low-fired, tin-glazed pottery, but was broadened to include any glazed pots. Similarly, the term faïence, tin-glazed earthenware, derives from the Italian city of Faenza, near Bologna, which was a great ceramics manufacturing center in the sixteenth century.

Italian potters in the Umbrian town of Deruta distinguished their work by a golden luster placed atop dark blue decoration on a white background. In Montelupo, a small village near Florence under the patronage of the Medicis, there were so many potters that the whole town was gainfully employed producing ceramics. But the most brilliant pottery of this period undoubtedly came from Gubbio, where luster was applied to multicolored pieces. As in Deruta, ceramists tended to use this technique particularly to glaze surface relief work. Gubbio, a small village near Assisi,

◀ **Italian Renaissance lusterware.** An eighteenth-century Deruta plate with a graceful figure of a woman in profile, commemorative written legend, and repeat-pattern floral border painted on a white ground, with a luster finish.

had previously been famous for its rescue from a killer wolf by Saint Francis. However, the fame that Gubbio enjoyed for this thirteenth-century miracle was eclipsed during the Renaissance by the magnificent lusterware produced there by Giorgio Andreoli. This master craftsman was given the title Lord of the Citadel by the duke of Urbino. Later, Pope Leo X, patron of Raphael and Michelangelo, exempted Andreoli from paying taxes for life, in tribute to his exceptional talents.

By the close of the sixteenth century, lusterware had lost its popularity, completely upstaged by porcelain, the exquisite new style of ceramics that came into the spotlight from the Orient. For the next few centuries, lusterware was relegated to obscurity until its rediscovery and resurgence in the nineteenth century.

◀ **Italian lusterware.** The front entrance of an old factory in Deruta, where fine lusterware has been produced for centuries.

▶ **Italian Renaissance lusterware.** Made in Deruta, this beautifully turned sixteenth-century majolica lidded vase has a golden luster finish.

Oriental Lusterware

A favored pottery technique devised in sixteenth-century China was a thick, metallic luster applied irregularly over the surface of an object, the very imperfection of the finish giving it an extraordinary beauty. During the same period, in Japan, oribe pottery, featuring a green metallic luster, was developed as tea-ceremony ware, the pieces often having irregular shapes.

English Lusterware

The Industrial Age of the nineteenth century ushered in a series of great international exhibitions to disseminate news of the latest technological wonders. Among the most important of these huge events were London's Crystal Palace Exhibition of 1851, and Barcelona's Universal Exhibition of 1888. Both laid special emphasis on new mass-produced, machine-made articles of various kinds and created instant public demand for them. But many people strongly resisted the trend toward machine-made goods supplanting finer workmanship and handcrafts. In England, a leading opponent was the eminent poet-artist William Morris, who had a decisive influence on the resurgence of traditional craftsmanship in general, and on lusterware pottery in particular. Another force in English design of the time was the artisan William de Morgan, who had used lusters on his work in glass. In 1882, following a fire that destroyed his studio, de Morgan relocated to be near Morris's workshops and dedicated himself increasingly to pottery. He devised an innovative process for producing brilliant blue and green glazes, which he used in creating decorative tiles for chimneys, walls, and the interiors of ships; the designs for these featured

► **Oriental lusterware.** Vessel of the Ch'ing dynasty with lustrous golden glaze.

floral, fish, and fanciful animal patterns. Following de Morgan's retirement in 1907, apprentices continued his work, and after his death in 1917, numerous craftsmen emulated his unique style.

At the dawn of the twentieth century, as demand continued to grow for wall tiles, an English manufacturing center was established near Manchester. The ceramist Abraham Lomax and chemist William Burton began research aimed at finding a crystalline glaze. They achieved their goal in 1903, and began producing their work at Pilkington's, a Lancaster company known for its artistic creations. With shapes and designs inspired by Persian and Chinese decoration, this distinctive pottery owed its popularity to its vibrantly colored glazes of vermilion, ultramarine blue, and silvery orange—three finishes that have made this lusterware an enduring favorite.

Another milestone in the history of English lusterware was an iridescent glaze created in 1905 and applied extensively by artists and designers during the next decades. In 1931, it was awarded the title Royal Lancaster by King George V. But soon thereafter, the English ceramics industry collapsed in the wake of the Great Depression and oncoming war.

▼ **English lusterware.** This small square saucer is part of a coffee set that was first covered in luster glaze, then finished with gold borders.

► **English lusterware.** A typical early-twentieth-century jug combines luster glaze and relief work in a style similar to the work of William de Morgan. Private collection.

Majolica and Faïence

As noted earlier, both of these names refer to tin-glazed earthenware. Given the popularity that this style of work enjoyed in Italy, it wasn't surprising that it was widely copied. At first, because imitators didn't know just how to achieve the luster effect, they used manganese compounds, and the decorative motifs were Moorish in style.

The name *majolica* originally applied to tin-glazed pottery imported from Spain to Italy via Majorca during the fifteenth century; the French term *faïence* derived from the popularity in sixteenth-century France of a type of majolica produced at the Faenza potteries in Italy that was characterized by a thick white glaze and fairly spare painted decoration (*Bianco di Faenza*). Although the two terms often are used interchangeably, today faïence is applied to all tin-glazed pottery, including French, Spanish, German, and Scandinavian wares in this category, whereas majolica is reserved only for Italian faïence pottery.

Faïence is customarily decorated by painting the design onto the underlying coat of unfired tin enamel. The piece is then submitted to a very hot firing. However, the faïence known as Delft, which originated in Holland in the seventeenth century, was decorated on top of a fired glaze in an attempt to imitate Chinese painting.

▲ **Majolica.** This multicolored, foliate-patterned plate bears the signature *Pesaro 1796* on its reverse side. Museo Internazionale delle Ceramiche, Italy. Cora Collection.

◄ **Faïence.** An elaborate commemorative design adorns this seventeenth-century vase with front pouring spout.

▼ **Majolica.** Although this plate was made in Talavera, Spain, the painting on it is Italian in style. Private collection.

Since cobalt oxide produces a beautiful blue that firing temperature does not affect, it's easy to see why this color has been so widely used in ceramic decoration, playing a fundamental role in Oriental pottery as well as Islamic and European. It should be noted that to achieve the color blue, copper oxide is also used.

Oriental Blue-and-White Ware

Cobalt pigments probably existed during the T'ang dynasty (A.D. 618–960), but little is known of their use during that period. It was in the fourteenth century that cobalt became important in ceramic adornment, and the blue-and-white tradition continues in China to the present day.

Some Chinese porcelains of this genre arrived in Europe before the sixteenth century. The quality of these first imports, with their mysterious, translucent, shiny designs painted in distant Cathay, was far superior to European and Near East pottery, which simply could not compete.

The process employed to achieve these beautiful finishes was applying ground cobalt to dry, unfired clay, which was then given a controlled, high-temperature firing to vitrify the glaze, paste, and color.

Early blue-and-white Japanese porcelains were somewhat crude. Of Korean inspiration, they are thought to have been introduced in the seventeenth century, but with the collapse of China's Ming dynasty, the flourishing Ch'eng-te Chen kilns stopped production. As a direct result, Japanese factories increased their number dramatically to cover the demand for blue-and-white ware sought by markets such as Holland, Persia, and India. Whereas earlier Japanese porcelain decoration had been spare and primitive, during the period of expansion, it evolved into very elaborate narrative designs. A single pattern often depicted people, animals, birds, pagodas, bridges—all in graceful landscape settings, carefully paint-

▶ **Japanese blue-and-white ware.** Note the unusual brown border on this Japanese plate decorated with a typical Chinese theme.

▼ **Blue-and-white heraldic plate.** Armorial insignia of this type were directly inspired by Ming dynasty Chinese porcelain and widely used throughout Europe. Private collection.

ed in many tones of blue against a pure white background. This thriving period of production, however, was not very long lived. It lasted only from 1653 to 1690; then the Japanese were driven out of business when Chinese emperor K'ang Hsi reorganized the kilns at Ch'eng-te Chen and recovered his old markets.

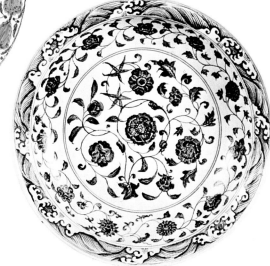

▲ **Chinese blue-and-white ware.** This fifteenth-century plate with a central floral, leaf, and vine pattern has stylized waves, a popular motif, adorning its rim.

▶ **Worcester blue-and-white ware.** Openwork and a classic Chinese landscape scene are combined on this fruit bowl produced in England.

◄ **European blue-and-white ware.** The delicately painted centered floral bouquet and border sprigs on this soup bowl typify northern European design. M. Pilar Navarro.

▼ **European blue-and-white ware.** Thick brushstrokes give this sixteenth-century bowl a provincial quality.

► **European blue-and-white ware**. As here, Spanish wine jugs of this sort often incorporate a poem or message, usually of a philosophical or moralizing nature.

▲ **European blue-and-white ware.** This eighteenth-century majolica piece is decorated with an allegorical scene painted in a range of blues.

Islamic Blue-and-White Ware

I n excavations carried out in Samarra, in north-central Iraq, small plates dating to the ninth century decorated with cobalt blue have been found. Since the history of Islamic pottery is largely unknown, further archaeological investigation may show that cobalt was in use even earlier.

European Blue-and-White Ware

T he various European attempts at replicating Oriental blue-and-white ware finally bore fruit with the development of Holland's famous faïence pottery in Delft, and later, with Germany's manufacture of blue-and-white porcelain in Meissen.

Dutch wares produced in Delft influenced Persian and Chinese ceramists, and also inspired the engravings of the seventeenth-century French ornament designer Daniel Marot. Curiously, while many aspects of the figures painted by European decorators conformed to Western norms, faces often had Oriental features and some designs freely mixed Chinese and European themes. Competing for the same markets, once German artisans succeeded in producing blue-and-white ware at Meissen, the output at Delft dropped, although the decorative styles of the two continued much along the same lines.

In England, there were several factories that supplied blue-and-white ware at lower prices, well within reach of middle-class purchasers. But for the privileged upper class, a factory in Chelsea manufactured limited editions of exclusive patterns at higher prices, though they, too, were generally decorated in the Chinese style based on floral motifs intermixed with English scenes.

Polychromatic palettes have long been applied to ceramics—from rough earthenware to fine porcelains—in many parts of the world. Perhaps the earliest artists of the dim past painted with only one or two colors, but nature's rich range of pigments was soon discovered, and the full spectrum has been beautifying ceramics for millennia.

Just how color and design are combined is what determines a particular ceramic style. Many styles established centuries ago are being adapted by present-day artisans, often with the same color choices of the originals that inspired them, as seen in the examples shown here.

▲ **Islamic style.** A very intricate repeat pattern of intertwined, geometric shapes, painted in a dozen colors, fully covers the surface of this serving platter of typical Islamic design. Private collection.

▶ **Oriental style.** Characteristic of vases from the Orient, the decoration on this example is painted in subtle shades of blues and reds accented with gold highlights in relief.

▼ **Porcelain.** These cups show the diversity of shapes and surface patterns characteristic of fine porcelain ware. The generous use of gold gives an elegant finish to the delicate floral and swag motifs painted in pastel tones.

The Kakiemon Style

This seventeenth-century Japanese style is named for the porcelain maker Sakaida Kakiemon, who is said to have introduced it to Japan from China in 1644. Much imitated by leading European factories, among them Meissen, Chelsea, and Chantilly, the style uses overglazed enamels in many colors, generally combined with gold and often arranged in asymmetrical patterns that have large areas left unadorned to show off the whiteness of the porcelain. Many variations of the style emerged, some of which can be identified by the date of manufacture or place of origin.

European versions copied Oriental narrative themes and gave strange names to some of them, such as *Gremlin in the Well,* depicting a complete legend in which a child makes a hole in the side of a large earthenware jar to save a friend who had fallen into it. Another pattern was called *Blazing Turtle,* showing the animal, the symbol of long life in Japan, with seaweed on its shell to symbolize its old age. *Phoenix* is a pattern honoring exotic Japanese "ho-ho" birds, always shown as a pair in flight. These designs and others with colorful Oriental themes stirred the imagination of the West and spread myths of the romantic paradise that the Far East was thought to be.

The Kakiemon style influenced ceramic decoration in Europe and China, as both areas were forced to compete with Japan.

▲ **Kakiemon style.** Eight beautiful glazes have been applied to this double-bowled vase with graceful long neck.

▼ **Kakiemon style.** An eighteenth-century octagonal plate combines exotic Oriental birds with a European floral swag pattern.

◀ **Kakiemon style.** This tall vase has a feature that is common to the genre: generous use of orange-reds and gold. Private collection.

The French style of china ware that is known today as Sèvres in fact was born in Vincennes, near Paris. Although the first experiments began in 1730, it was not until 1753 that thriving production was in place, relocated in Sèvres, with the identifying royal symbol of crossed *L*s stamped on the underside of each piece. A town near the River Seine between Paris and Versailles, Sèvres took over European leadership from Meissen under the patronage of Louis XV and Madame de Pompadour, who gave the porcelain brand a fashionable and semi-monopolistic position. The date of production was added below the crossed *L*s, with the letter *A* corresponding to the year 1753 and the rest of the letters of the alphabet being used for the following years. The hallmark of Sèvres products was to undergo one further modification when in 1768 a crown was added over the crossed *L*s.

At first Meissen and Chantilly designs were copied, but little by little, Sèvres acquired a character all its own and soon became unmistakable for the richness of its floral paintings, often executed on deep ground colors—dark blue, turquoise, yellowish pink, or green. Human figures and birds were painted with exquisite precision, and the elaborate gilding used for trim greatly influenced rococo furnishings and goldsmithing of the same period.

Sèvres dinner services became especially famous. In 1783, Louis XVI ordered a 445–piece dinner service for the Palace of Versailles, which was produced over a period of twenty years.

◀ **Sèvres.** A plate belonging to Catherine the Great of Russia bears the imperial insignia and commemorative portraits.

▼ **Sèvres.** Tête-à-tête service with elaborate medallions encircling romantic figures, a profusion of gold, and garlands of flowers all reveal the Sèvres style. Private collection.

27

Nature-Inspired Ceramic Design

Nature has been turned to as a source of inspiration in ceramics decoration for centuries. Early Chinese pottery created for funereal rites often took on abstracted animal and human forms. Figure drawings often densely covered surfaces with little background space left empty.

As investigation into nature's wonders grew in the eighteenth century, environmental motifs for decoration in general and for pottery in particular enjoyed increased popularity throughout Europe. Although Meissen pieces of botanical motifs are earlier than those produced by Chelsea, the latter became the most famous worldwide. They are popularly known as *Sir Hans Sloane Dinner Service,* named after an eminent British physician-naturalist and leading collector of the period.

Many ceramic decorations included butterflies and other insects to give the designs more realism. But it should be pointed out that there is a difference between the accuracy of the plants when considered individually and the composition as a whole, which was largely a product of the artist's imagination.

At first, other British manufacturers imitated the Chelsea style, emphasizing botanical decoration, but in time developed forms of their own expression, even though none ever achieved the beauty of their prototype's products. The botanical style reached its zenith in Derby at the beginning of the nineteenth century with meticulously rendered replications of roses, tulips, and other species. The super-realistic naturalist style then lost its popularity, and although it was never completely abandoned, it has never again enjoyed its former great success.

◄ **Animal design.** A deer running through ferns typifies motifs used on ceramics that catered to European tastes for scenes from nature. The monochrome paint is applied flatly, giving a bold, silhouetted look to the animal and border vine. Private collection.

◄ **Single floral.** Botanical painting on porcelain is particularly elegant when a single flower such as this tulip has lifelike detailing.

► **Multiple floral.** Realistically painted, casually placed chrysanthemums flow beautifully with the shape of this shallow porcelain Limoges serving piece. M. Pilar Navarro.

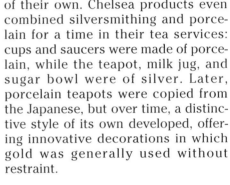

Although Chinese pottery and porcelain have long been regarded as primary sources of inspiration for ceramists the world over, it must be noted that Chinese potters, in turn, owe much of their art to various cultures and crafts that contributed shapes, pigments, and decorative styles to their work. High on the list of influence from other sources is the impact of goldsmithing on porcelain embellishment. Before elaborating on that fact, a brief overview of intercultural and interart influences follows.

The three periods that determine the history of Chinese pottery are the T'ang, Ming, and Ch'ing dynasties. Spanning a dozen centuries between the seventh and the nineteenth A.D., developments in ceramic design during this broad time frame relied in part on contributions from other times and places. Even during the Shang dynasty (1766–1122 B.C.), earthenware copies were already being made of bronze pieces, a tradition that was to continue for centuries.

The prosperity and opulence of the T'ang dynasty brought to that court commodities from far-off lands that impacted on pottery manufacture in one way or another. For instance, silver bowls and other imported Hellenic pieces were copied by potters.

The Ming period also saw an increase in commerce, with new objects arriving along routes that skirted the Gobi Desert. These goods gave rise to new shapes and designs that were adapted by Chinese potters—most significantly, the placing of blue and red pigments under glaze, a technique that was to revolutionize the design and color of pottery. Strangely enough, such pieces were made only for export to Europe, since they were unpopular among the Chinese, who regarded them as being crude.

Foreign craftsmanship impacted on Chinese manufacture during certain eras of the Ch'ing dynasty as a result of active seafaring exchange with the Dutch, English, and Portuguese. Styles such as Baroque and Rococo were well received in official Chinese circles, although native cultural tradi-

▶ **Rococo sugar bowl.** Delicate flowers and tiny butterflies, painted in soft colors, are scattered about this gracefully shaped piece. Matte-gold accents highlight the handles and lid. M. Pilar Navarro.

tions of the Ming period were always preferred.

In Europe, after discovering the formula for making porcelain, at first ceramists copied all sorts of Oriental pieces, but very soon new directions were taken in decorating the recently discovered material. This is when goldsmithing made its big impact, literally and figuratively, as objects of the precious metal were not only copied for their splendid designs; some gold filigree work was pressed into the porcelain clay to produce relief work. This is precisely what happened with Meissen and Chelsea

▲ **Limoges.** A romantic moment is captured in a gold painting that pops out brilliantly against its cobalt-blue background.

products until they developed styles of their own. Chelsea products even combined silversmithing and porcelain for a time in their tea services: cups and saucers were made of porcelain, while the teapot, milk jug, and sugar bowl were of silver. Later, porcelain teapots were copied from the Japanese, but over time, a distinctive style of its own developed, offering innovative decorations in which gold was generally used without restraint.

▶ **Rosenthal.** Single and double pansies alternate in this repeat pattern encircling a porcelain butter dish with lid. Gold decoration is reserved for borders and handles.

Twentieth-Century Ceramists

As discussed earlier (under the heading "Oriental and English Lusterware"), toward the end of the nineteenth century, many artists and thinkers banded together in opposition to decadent tastes of the period. Prominent in this movement was the ceramist William de Morgan, who tried to return to older, more traditional values by making his pieces with the same beauty and quality as ceramics fashioned during the Renaissance. Known as the Arts and Crafts Movement and founded at the same time as Art Nouveau was being internationalized, its influence on pottery was widely felt.

Another important figure at this time was Bernard Leach, a British potter who was born in Hong Kong, trained in the Oriental ceramic tradition, and after settling in England, established Leach Pottery of St. Ives, which greatly influenced contemporary ceramic design. His unique style was based on a combination of Oriental and medieval English themes.

Hans Coper arrived in England in 1939, fleeing from Nazism. Although his formal training was not very extensive, he was employed by the Lucie Ries studio, and his work

▲ **Textural style.** The finish on this chunky vessel is what draws both the eye and the hand to it, as its rough texture invites touch.

showed such skill and imagination that by 1951, he was producing his own collection of pieces for the firm. He followed no particular tradition, but his work can be identified easily by its own definite style, and the fact that no two pieces are ever the same.

Another contributor to breakthrough styles at the beginning of this century was Catalan ceramist Josep Aragay, who had a hand in ushering in a *Novecento* style, the Italian term for twentieth-century art in general and the name of a movement that aimed at reviving Renaissance approaches to craftsmanship. Tiles decorated by Aragay adorn the beautiful Portal de l'Angel in Barcelona. After 1925, he stopped decorating tiles and concentrated instead on creating shapes that mix Spanish and Italian styles.

Antoni Serra, also a Catalan, started out as a painter, but after working in a ceramics factory and attending some courses in Sèvres, he set up a ceram-

ics workshop in Barcelona, producing work with a distinct modernist flair.

Two other ceramists of note whose work interpreted traditional styles in contemporary terms were Josep Llorens, who focused more on shape than surface adornment, and Antoni Cumellas, who devoted himself to finding numerous new contours for jugs. Also a muralist who worked in relief, he focused on perfecting the use of different clays, enamels, and the kiln. Cumellas received the prestigious Gold Medal at the 1951 Triennale de Milán, and ever since this international recognition, Catalan pottery has occupied a prominent position in the world.

◀ **Bernard Leach design.** Shaped on the wheel and simply glazed to make the relief work stand out, this piece by Bernard Leach combines incised and pinched details to produce a handsome repeat pattern.

▶ **Josep Aragay design.** This illustrative piece celebrating the harvest is rendered in a Mediterranean style, with some obvious Florentine influences.

Monochromatic

The Chinese were undoubtedly the potters who reached the highest standards when glazing pots in one color, whereas in the West, ceramics or porcelain were generally regarded as being nothing more than a surface on which to paint a multicolored picture.

Given European taste, little Chinese monochrome production reached the West, although some pieces were transported to Egypt and the Near East during the Middle Ages.

In terms of glazes for monochrome work, there has long been an assortment from which to choose; they are often made as a mixture with ground metallic oxides. The bisque, or unglazed ceramic, was nearly always decorated with its design before being glazed. Sculpted ornaments or shapes were also added before firing the piece, which was then left to dry in the sun. Semitransparent glazes accumulated in relief patterns and acquired a darker color, depending on how thickly the glaze had been applied.

With some glaze pastes, an almost translucent, extraordinarily shiny whiteness could be achieved with a completely smooth surface.

At the end of the seventeenth century, under the guidance of the Manchurians, there was a return to the golden age of monochrome, although techniques used were more developed than they had been under earlier dynasties. During this period, single-color pottery was also more widely accepted in Europe. The most sought-after glazes were ruby red, grayish yellow, and porcelain white. Precious metals were often included in glaze mixtures to make their beauty stand out even more. Generally, monochrome porcelain and ceramics find their most enthusiastic audience among sophisticated collectors and other experts in the field.

► **Monochromatic earthenware.** The contemporary Catalan ceramist Antoni Serra created this "pleated" trivet. Its one-color finish emphasizes the contours of its imaginative shape. Private collection.

Raku

The Japanese word for "enjoyment," *raku* is the term used to describe a style of molded tea ware, usually of irregular shape and texture. The first raku was created in Kyoto in the sixteenth century, and its production continues to this day.

The British ceramist Bernard Leach introduced raku to Europe early in this century. Fired at very low temperature and covered with thick lead glaze, raku differs technically from other types of ceramics in that, once pieces have reached the required temperature in the kiln, they must be immediately submerged in water. Extraordinary effects are produced in raku ware due to this process of reduction and oxidization. Special kilns are often used to achieve the desired effect. Raku glaze may be of any color, but traditionally, the preference is for dark hues.

The word "unique" can truly be applied to raku, because exactly how a piece will turn out is unpredictable, and every piece is somewhat different from the next. The technique has the great advantage of allowing correction; if the finish is not the one desired, the whole operation can be repeated by putting the piece back into the kiln to go through the process again.

▲ **Monochromatic porcelain.** The harmony of a pale rose and cream-colored glaze produces a monochromatic effect on this porcelain side plate manufactured by Rosenthal. M. Pilar Navarro.

► **Raku.** A rough-textured, sixteenth-century Japanese raku vase made on the wheel typifies the exceptional, one-of-kind effects achieved using this method.

MATERIALS AND EQUIPMENT

Every art medium and every craft has its own set of techniques and standards, and decorating ceramics is no exception to the rule. A particularly diverse craft, ceramics ornamentation takes in many different methods, with specific tools and equipment required for each. This chapter presents essential materials from which to choose in setting up a studio or work area reserved in your home for practicing this craft.

Not every decorating technique is compatible with every ceramic form, so it's important to review the full range of possibilities before deciding which materials you'll need for the ceramic piece you wish to embellish, be it bisque-fired, glazed earthenware, or glazed porcelain.

Once you have familiarized yourself with materials and equipment, you'll be much better prepared to follow information about the wide variety of techniques employed, and the step-by-step demonstrations for many of them presented in the final section of this book.

When you add your own artistry to the background knowledge of tools and techniques that you'll acquire from these pages, you will be on your way to creating originals for your personal pleasure or to delight others with lovely and thoughtful gifts.

The term *ceramics* is applied to many materials that receive decoration successfully: white clay, red clay, glazed red clay (all raw or bisque-fired), glazed earthenware, and glazed porcelain.

The person who decorates the piece is often not the same person who makes it. Most often, artists will buy unadorned ceramic objects from crafts stores and apply their own "signature" embellishment. Many hobbyists and professionals work on old pieces of porcelain, a plate or soup bowl, for example, which can be decorated artistically, provided the piece is white or pale-colored and has no cracks in it. But note that prior to painting any old glazed piece, all surface impurities must be removed by placing the piece in boiling water containing about a 5-percent concentration of borax.

Once you've acquired the confidence that practice and experience brings, there's great satisfaction to be had from the whole process: finding an appealing ceramic piece to decorate; imagining the various motifs that you might use, then settling on your choice; executing the design work, often letting spontaneous, unexpected effects guide you; and finally, proudly admiring the finished object taken out of the kiln after its last firing.

If tiles are to be developed into a mural, blank tiles can be bought for decorating, or if the project calls for a wall mural set at different planes, ceramists often make tiles themselves with built-in relief effects.

With the great variety of ceramics offered for decoration, and the myriad techniques available, the combinations are almost endless.

▶ **Engobe coating.** This raw jug is covered in engobe, a mixture of fine clay and water applied to earthenware as a support for glaze or enamel.

▼ **Earthenware set.** Raw earthenware pieces are covered in engobe to conceal the red tone of the clay, providing a light background for surface adornment.

▲ Porcelain plate. An ideal finish for this plate would be delicate florals painted in the empty spaces between the relief pattern on the rim.

► Earthenware pitcher. Covered in engobe, this pitcher has a shape that invites a bold surface design to emphasize its interesting contours.

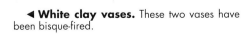

▲ Red earthenware cup and saucer. The first firing of a raw clay object to harden it prior to glazing is known as bisque-firing. The unglazed cup and saucer shown here are bisque ware.

◄ White clay vases. These two vases have been bisque-fired.

As with many avocations, ceramics decoration often begins in a corner of the family room or on the proverbial kitchen table—perhaps a better choice with its added advantage of a handy water supply. But as you spend more time with your craft, chances are you'll want to have a permanent space set up for it—ideally, a room devoted exclusively to ceramics decoration. There are no set rules about how to arrange a ceramist's studio, but it's important to establish a workplace with bright, preferably natural, light, ideally facing north. Good ventilation and a nearby water supply are also necessary. By adding a large table, a comfortable chair, and several shelves, you'll be ready to start decorating.

The kinds of tools and materials needed vary a great deal according to the technique involved. The following list of materials and equipment covers all the techniques included in this book. Of course, to begin your decoration work, you won't need everything—just those materials required for the particular technique or techniques you choose for starters.

▲ **Ceramics decoration studio.** This sketch shows an ideal basic set-up for working efficiently and comfortably: 1) worktable with storage drawers; 2) adjustable chair on wheels; 3) cart or small wheeled table for materials used most often while working; 4) sink; 5) shelves for reference books; 6) shelves for unfinished pieces; 7) window with direct sunlight.

▶ **Ceramist at work.** As shown in this photo of the author in her studio, a large room is unnecessary, even for a professional. Any space with proper lighting can be fitted out as needed. Venetian blinds are drawn on one window to control excessive light in this case.

Materials

You will come to know this array of basic materials well in your ceramics decoration work. It is not an exhaustive list, but does contain a selection of the most commonly used items. For handy reference, many terms used are more fully explained in the Glossary at the back of this book.

◀ **Engobe.** Semi-liquid clay paste for relief decoration, it can be colored by adding any of a wide range of powdered pigments to the mixture. In its natural cream tone, it is used to hide the color of a piece—red clay, for example—so that painted decoration can be applied.

◀ **Hydrofluoric acid.** Used for etching; you must handle it with great care, wearing rubber gloves to prevent burns.

◀ **Slip.** Clay dissolved in water to a creamy consistency and used as an adhesive to affix parts, such as handles. Depending on use, slip may or may not contain a deflocculent—a substance that prevents rapid settling and lessens the amount of water required.

◀ **Liquid asphalt.** Used as a protective layer (ground) in the etching technique.

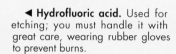

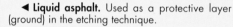

▶ **Graphite powder.** Easily obtained by scraping the tip of a soft-lead pencil with a sharp knife; used for marking perforations in stenciling.

▼ **Wax.** (Lower left) Used as resist to reserve areas of decoration, it repels moisture, then disappears during the first stages of firing.

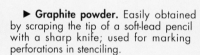

▼ **Ceramics clay.** Raw red or white clay; many grades can be bought, according to your preference: earthenware, stoneware, porcelain, etc.

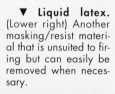

▼ **Liquid latex.** (Lower right) Another masking/resist material that is unsuited to firing but can easily be removed when necessary.

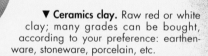

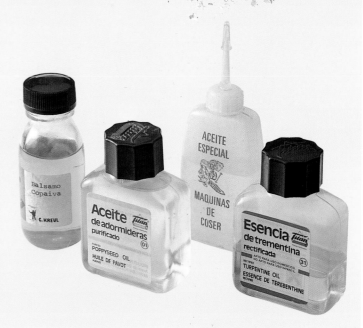

▲ Decals. Available in many motifs, decals are handy for creating elaborate designs effortlessly when decorating white-glazed porcelain pieces.

▲ Tapes and self-stick papers. Tapes are for protecting and masking off one area of a ceramic piece while working on others. Decorative geometric patterns can be cut out from sheets of self-stick paper.

► India ink. Used for drawing on porcelain.

▼ Turpentine. A solvent for cleaning brushes used with India ink and other oil-based materials, as well as for thinning oil-based paints.

► Powdered sugar. Used in the *cuerda seca* (dry line) technique, in which colors painted on porcelain are separated with a fine line of powder.

▼ Alcohol. Be sure to use only denatured alcohol to clean brushes used for gold and lusters, and for cleaning porcelain before painting.

► Mediums. These are mixed with pigments to make paints used for decorating; they include water, poppyseed oil, gum turpentine, and other liquids. The mixture should be of a creamy consistency for easy application and smooth brushwork.

◀ **Rags, paper towels, napkins.** For brushes and general clean-up; for wiping ceramic pieces, paper is preferable to cloth, which may leave threads on clay.

◀ **Fine-grain sandpaper.** For polishing paint finishes on kaolin, which is a fine white clay used in making porcelain.

▲ **Dropper.** Useful for applying small quantities of liquid.

▼ **Silk or other cloth.** For polishing ceramic surfaces; the type of cloth depends on the desired effect.

▲ **Gold finish.** Solvents and burnish for gold.

▶ **Paints.** All of the materials shown on page 39 are paints. They are categorized as underglazes, glazes, and overglazes. Paints are mineral pigments available in different forms: powder which needs to be mixed with a medium; sticks (pastel); cakes (similar to pan watercolors); and mixed and ready-to-use paints. There are many brands on the market, offering a vast range of products to suit different techniques and color needs. Some ready-made paints produce beautiful effects.

▲ **Transfer tracing paper.** For precision tracing of designs on a ceramic surface, be sure to use design transfer paper, not ordinary office carbon paper, which will leave smears on clay and may muddy paint and glaze colors.

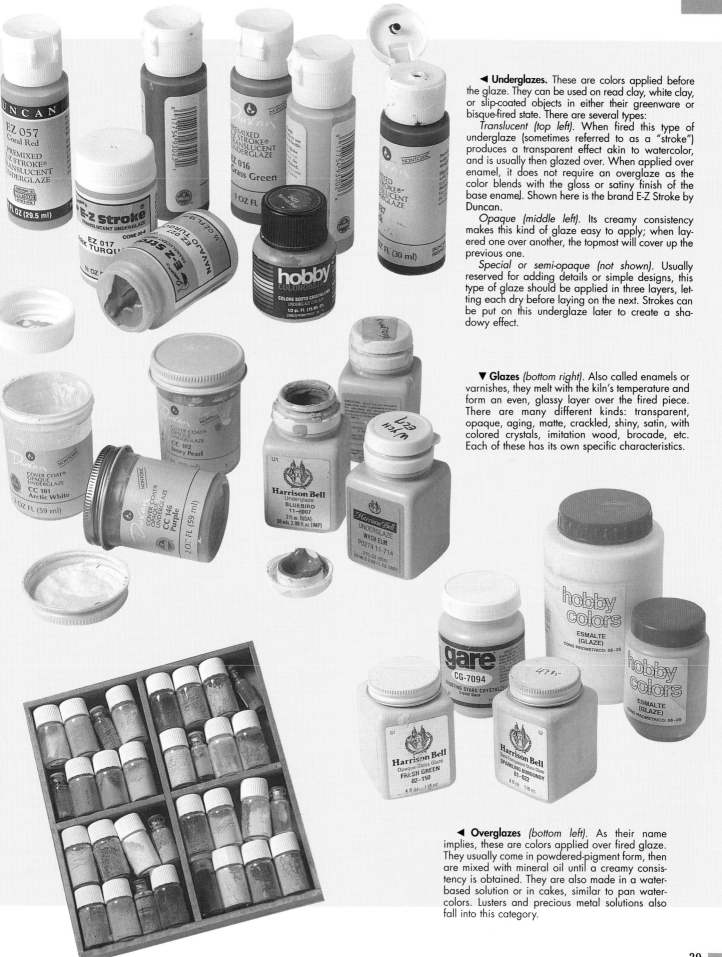

◄ Underglazes. These are colors applied before the glaze. They can be used on read clay, white clay, or slip-coated objects in either their greenware or bisque-fired state. There are several types:

Translucent (top left). When fired this type of underglaze (sometimes referred to as a "stroke") produces a transparent effect akin to watercolor, and is usually then glazed over. When applied over enamel, it does not require an overglaze as the color blends with the gloss or satiny finish of the base enamel. Shown here is the brand E-Z Stroke by Duncan.

Opaque (middle left). Its creamy consistency makes this kind of glaze easy to apply; when layered one over another, the topmost will cover up the previous one.

Special or semi-opaque (not shown). Usually reserved for adding details or simple designs, this type of glaze should be applied in three layers, letting each dry before laying on the next. Strokes can be put on this underglaze later to create a shadowy effect.

▼ Glazes *(bottom right).* Also called enamels or varnishes, they melt with the kiln's temperature and form an even, glassy layer over the fired piece. There are many different kinds: transparent, opaque, aging, matte, crackled, shiny, satin, with colored crystals, imitation wood, brocade, etc. Each of these has its own specific characteristics.

◄ Overglazes *(bottom left).* As their name implies, these are colors applied over fired glaze. They usually come in powdered-pigment form, then are mixed with mineral oil until a creamy consistency is obtained. They are also made in a water-based solution or in cakes, similar to pan watercolors. Lusters and precious metal solutions also fall into this category.

Equipment

T he equipment and tools shown and described on these pages are the ones you will find most efficient for creating handsome ceramics decoration.

▶ **Sponges.** Coarse or fine, depending on your purpose, sponges are used for applying backgrounds or filling in stencils, and for wiping dust from bisque-fired pieces after sanding. Sponges also create interesting textured effects on the surface of a piece.

Rubber stamps. For imprinting designs in clay, stamps can be purchased ready-made or custom-designed.

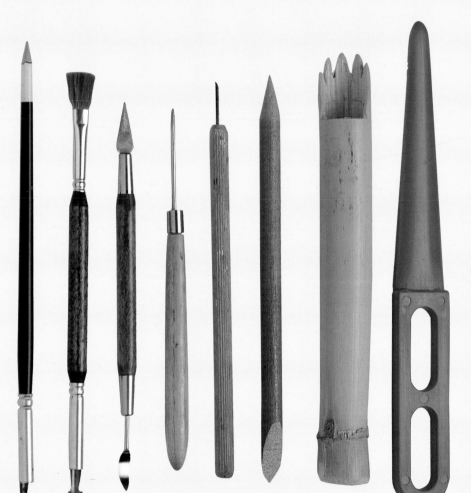

▲ **Stencils.** For tracing designs onto pieces, commercially bought stencils can be used again and again, but require careful cleaning to remove traces of paint after each use.

◀ **Marking tools.** Knives, lancets, stilettos, punches, and other instruments used for incising, cutting, scratching, and marking clay. This group includes metal, bamboo, and wooden tips.

▼ **Stamping dies.** Cylinders with designs to be stamped into leatherhard clay.

▶ **Glazed white tile.** As a palette for mixing colors, this or any piece of glass will do, with a sheet of white paper placed underneath to distinguish the hues.

▲ **Glass jars.** For cleaning brushes, recycled food jars of all kinds are useful.

◀ **Eraser.** At far left is one specially made for erasing from porcelain; next to it, an ordinary eraser with brush for bisque-fired pieces.
Pencils. For tracing/drawing, soft pencils are best on porcelain.
Nibs. In addition to the one shown, other sizes are available.
Gold pen. Mostly for applying fine, continuous lines, this tool holds a small amount of liquid gold that flows out through a tiny opening. It's a smaller version of a tool made for applying engobe.

▼ **Droppers, horns, syringes.** For applying engobe in relief; before these ball-shaped tools were invented, real ox horns were used.

◀ **Spatulas.** In many different sizes, none has a specific function. Flexible metal blades are efficient for mixing and thinning colors.

▶ **Large bucket or pan.** Preferably made of polyethylene or propylene, for holding hydrofluoric acid when etching.

41

▲ **Wire.** Steel wire affixed to wooden handles, for cutting clay.

▶ **Brushes.** For stripes or veined effects, the paired brush/comb is a handy implement. Brushes also produce appealing textured effects.

▲ **Scissors.** Practical for general studio use and specifically for cutting paper patterns, conventional or battery-operated scissors will do.

◀ **Combs.** Metal, bamboo, or wooden combs for engraving clay with regularly or irregularly spaced fluted patterns. The hardness of the clay should be considered when you are choosing an implement.

▼ **Pipettes.** Not used, as might be expected, for dripping out small amounts of liquid, but for blowing air onto a concentrated spot. A straw or any tube can be substituted, such as the empty ballpoint pen in the photo.

▼ ▶ **Brushes.** Of the many sizes, shapes, and quality of brushes available, sable are considered the best, although for ceramics, squirrel and other animal hairs are equally usable. Which style brush you choose is a matter of personal choice, and you'll probably find that even if you stock many kinds, one or two will become the favorites you rely on most. Still, it's useful to have an assortment on hand. Various brush types and sizes are shown here. Brush sizes range from #00 (smallest) to #16 (largest). Here's a summary of brush styles and their uses, and sizes you might need for ceramics decoration:

Rounds. For painting everything from fine curlicues to filling in broad areas of color: #2, 4, 6, 8.

Outliners. Rounds for painting fine outlines: #00, 0, 1.

Flats. For broad or hard-edge strokes: #2, 4, 6, 8, 10, 12.

Brights. Modified flats with stubbier hairs for more controlled strokes: #4, 6, 10.

Filberts. Flat brush with rounded tip, makes thin to thick strokes: #2, 4, 6.

Angles. Diagonal shape provides point and flat edge for thin to thick brushwork: #4, 6, 10.

Fan blenders. As its name implies, a fan-shaped brush for blending and special effects: a few sizes, usually unnumbered.

Wide brushes. Rounds for cleaning bisque-fired work: #14, 16.

Brushes used with underglazes or glazes must be cleaned with water immediately after use, paying special attention to removing all paint particles near the ferrule, the metal collar that holds the bristles. Be careful not to leave brushes upright in a container in solvent, as bristles will become deformed and unusable. Brushes used for India ink should be cleaned with turpentine, while those used for lusters, gold, and other metals should be rinsed out with alcohol or a special solvent.

Materials summary. With the information as to materials and equipment reviewed thus far, and the section that follows regarding kilns, you will be prepared to practice any of the techniques covered in this book.

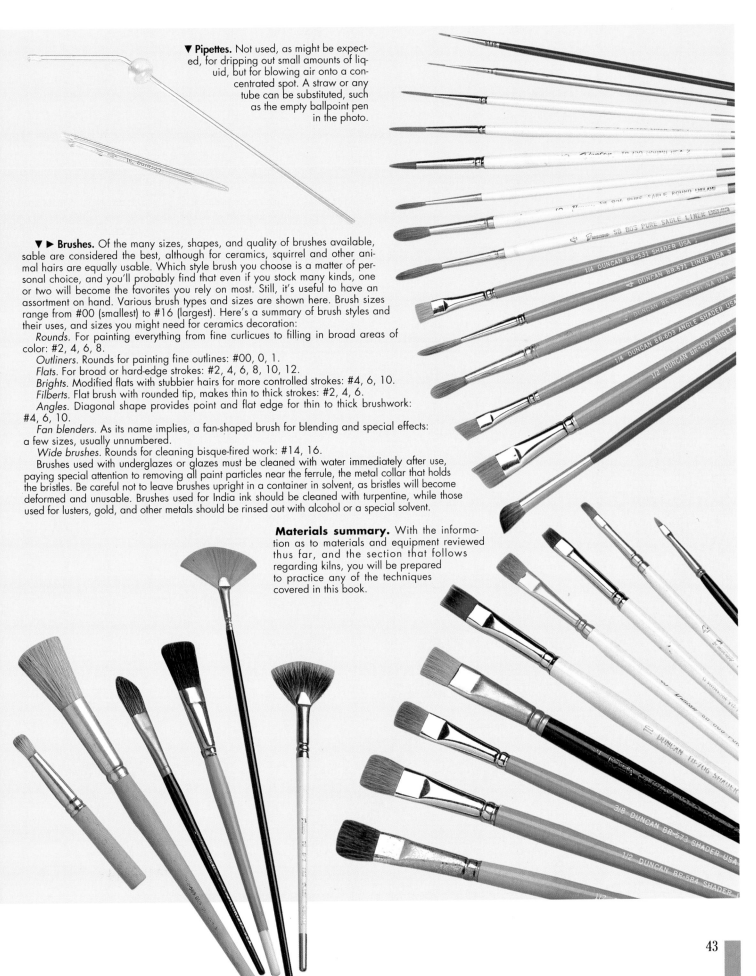

Kilns

Firing in the kiln is the very last stage of decoration. Virtually every ceramist faces that exciting moment when the kiln door is opened to reveal the finished piece—a moment of great apprehension, anticipation, and hope.

Many hobbyists engaged in decorating ceramics do not own a kiln. Pieces ready for firing can be taken to ceramics studios where such services are offered. To familiarize you with the various kilns in use, here's a brief summary of their types. The most modern kilns operate under the same principles as the oldest ones, the main difference being how they are powered.

Fire Kilns

Using fire to bake pottery is an ancient process. Kilns of the past and present include those fired by wood, coal, oil, or gas.

Updraft Kiln

The fire is in the lower section, and heat enters the kiln through a grating, to fire the pieces inside. Smoke escapes through a chimney at the top. This is an old style of kiln.

Downdraft Kiln

In this type of kiln, flames reach the top, spread downward toward the floor, then out through the chimney. This system is used in kilns with several levels, each with a different function.

Crossdraft Kiln

The firebox is in the lower front part, but separated from the chamber by a thin partition that stops ash and other impurities from reaching the pieces stacked inside. Flames cross the pieces horizontally until they reach the chimney. Oriental kilns work on this principle.

Muffle Kiln

In this style, flames do not come into direct contact with the pieces, which are protected in an inner chamber called a muffle.

	Seger cones	Orton cones	
Nº	Temperature °C	Temperature °C	Temperature °F
022	600	600	1112
021	650	614	1137
020	670	635	1175
019	690	683	1261
018	710	717	1323
017	730	747	1377
016	750	792	1458
015 a	790	804	1479
014 a	815	838	1540
013 a	835	852	1566
012 a	855	884	1623
011 a	880	894	1641
010 a	900	894	1641
09 a	920	923	1693
08 a	940	955	1751
07 a	960	984	1803
06 a	980	999	1830
05 a	1000	1046	1915
04 a	1020	1060	1940
03 a	1040	1101	2014
02 a	1060	1120	2048
01 a	1080	1137	2079
1 a	1100	1154	2109
2 a	1120	1162	2124
3 a	1140	1168	2134
4 a	1160	1186	2167
5 a	1180	1196	2185
6 a	1200	1222	2232
7	1230	1240	2264
8	1250	1263	2305
9	1280	1280	2336
10	1300	1305	2381
11	1320	1315	2399
12	1350	1326	2419
13	1380	1346	2455
14	1410	1366	2491
15	1435	1431	2608

◀ **Firing-guide table.** Pyrometric cones by Seger, a German firm, and Orton, an American firm, are rated here. Reference numbers of pyramid-shaped cones (examples shown below) are in the left column of table; equivalent temperatures in centigrade and Fahrenheit indicate the amount of heat at which the cones will soften and bend.

▼ **Pyrometric cones.** Three-sided pyramids used for testing when firing ceramic pieces. For greater accuracy, three cones are used. The middle one indicates the desired temperature.

Electric Kilns

Shown are the kilns best suited to a home studio. They do not require a chimney and are simple to use. If you do not have a kiln (a kitchen stove does not reach the required temperature) and are thinking of buying one, here are a few tips about how they work.

When you fire paint, you must subject it to controlled heat for a certain period of time until it reaches a temperature where the paint melts and fuses with the underlying surface, be it the clay or a subsequent glaze.

An electric kiln will come with a set of operating instructions, making it easy to use and explaining how to stack the pieces inside. The exterior dimension of the kiln is insignificant; it's the interior space that counts. You need about 15–20 square inches (40–50 cm) of height, width, and depth, a sufficient capacity for the most usual jobs.

Pyrometric cones (shown on the previous page) are used to measure the temperature. Proper control is obtained by used three cones in a line, the middle one indicating the desired temperature. The gradation of these cones is slightly different, according to the country of origin: Orton cones are used in the United States, Staffordshire cones in Great Britain, and Seger cones, from Germany, are used throughout Europe.

◄ **Top-loading electric kiln.** Highly practical and economical to use, this model has heating elements in two of its inner walls and can reach temperatures of up to 2305 degrees Fahrenheit (1263 degrees centigrade). An added advantage is that all the pieces can be seen at a glance to check that they are not touching, thus avoiding their sticking to one another during firing.

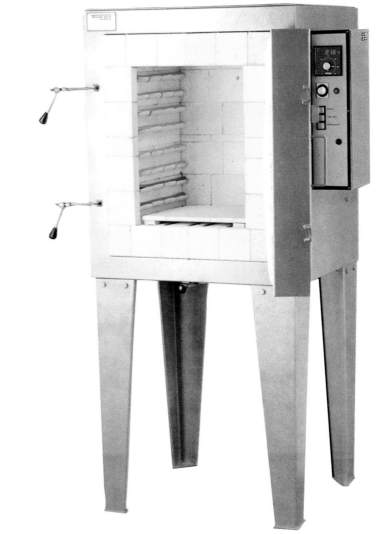

► **Front-loading kiln.** An easy-to-use kiln, this is the type I usually work with. Heating elements are set into the side walls. It is equipped with a platinum-rhodium thermo element (pyrometer) and an easy-to-use automatic regulating system. It can reach temperatures of up to about 2450 degrees Fahrenheit (1340 degrees centigrade). This type of kiln is one of the safest, most versatile, durable, and simple to operate.

Firing temperatures in studio kilns range from 1112 degrees Fahrenheit (600 degrees centigrade) for cone 022, to 2232 degrees Fahrenheit (1222 degrees centigrade) for cone 6.

Most electric kilns, however, are equipped with a thermostat to regulate the temperature. There are even fully automatic kilns that require no supervision during firing.

For bisque-fired ware or modeled pieces, no space need be left between them in the kiln, because any contact they have during firing will not cause damage. This is not the case with glazed or enameled pieces, which should never touch; air should be free to circulate around them. If they touch, the glaze would fuse them together, making it impossible to separate pieces without breakage. For the same reason it is also not advisable to place the pieces directly on the floor of the kiln. The melted glaze could run, and the piece would then be stuck to it. To prevent this from happening, different types of supports are used: stilts, props, and spurs, shown on page 47.

When loading the kiln, the finish determines how the pieces are arranged. The vapor released by certain glazes during firing may affect others, so much so that red enamels, for example, should not be fired for several hours after green enamels, as the red color could be affected.

If pieces decorated with an underglaze and a transparent glaze finish

◀ **Kiln arrangement.** Objects must be positioned carefully in the kiln; glazed pieces must not touch one another.

are fired at the same time as enameled pieces, the latter should be placed at the top of the kiln and the glazed items at the bottom.

After they have been fired, pieces should be left in the kiln until you can remove them without burning your hands. Otherwise, the sudden change in temperature could produce cracks or even breakage.

Although operating the kiln and remembering these several important points may take some time to master, the effort will more than pay off in the satisfaction you'll feel when you see your completed work.

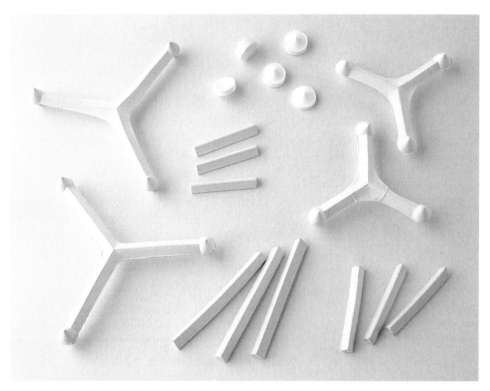

▲ **Stilts, props, spurs.** These are small supports on which glazed pieces are rested in the kiln. Stilts are Y-shaped, with three pointed ends. Props are triangular and measure an inch or two (two-three cm) in length. Spurs are cone-shaped, about three-eighths of an inch (one cm) high.

◀ **Plate racks.** Very handy if you are firing many plates together.

▶ **Tile racks.** Stackable tile racks that require little space and promote circulation of heat around the pieces.

◀ **Shelves or bats.** Used for resting pieces on and for creating different levels for loading, they are generally made of clay with a high aluminum content or of other materials that have high thermal resistance.

▼ **Pillars and props.** Supports for the bats or stacking shelves.

DECORATING TECHNIQUES

While this book deals with ornamenting ceramic objects once they have been formed, we can't separate surface decoration entirely from modeling. The moment the ceramist begins to shape an object, an aspect of its decoration has already begun. The choice of clay, its texture, shape, finish, and color are all important factors to take into account when you make your surface decorating decisions. So you are, in effect, the co-creator of each piece you decorate, embellishing the artisan's work—be it rough, unglazed earthenware, delicate porcelain, or a range of styles in between.

Adding Three-Dimensional Decoration

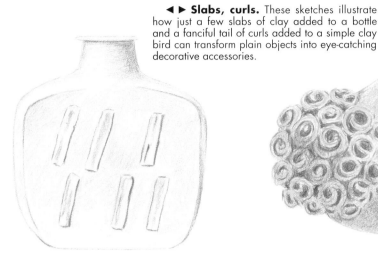

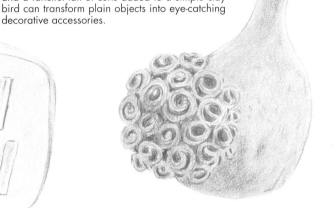

◀ ▶ **Slabs, curls.** These sketches illustrate how just a few slabs of clay added to a bottle and a fanciful tail of curls added to a simple clay bird can transform plain objects into eye-catching decorative accessories.

◀ **Relief.** The delicate relief work, white swirls on purple stripes, enhances this shell-shaped, rose-patterned porcelain.

▼ **Relief.** Fine gold relief outline, commonly seen on Oriental ceramics, heightens the beauty of this Japanese vase.

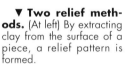

▼ **Two relief methods.** (At left) By extracting clay from the surface of a piece, a relief pattern is formed.

By adding clay to the surface of the piece, another type of relief pattern is formed.

Applications

Decorating by superimposing elements on an existing piece may be as simple as affixing a slither of clay applied with slip or a complete and complex sculpted design, such as the familiar relief of Wedgwood pottery. Three-dimensional elements can be applied to a surface by hand or by mold. The end result often looks the same, but using a mold offers the advantage of being able to produce multiple or coordinated pieces with the same decorative motif. Molds are made of fired clay or plaster; the latter wears away relatively quickly.

The clay pieces you attach to a given object may be of different sizes, shapes, and colors. In addition to decorative applications, functional additions may be made, such as adding handles to a bowl, but note that when appendages protrude too much, it's harder to make them adhere and cracks may occur.

A few strokes of clay slip brushed onto the support and to the back of the application is sufficient for adhesion. Any surplus slip (no matter how little) must be removed with caution, using a very fine brush.

Relief

In its broadest sense, relief is any type of decoration that projects from a flat surface. *High relief* is sculpture that extends far in front of its surface; *bas-relief,* or *low relief,* projects only slightly, such as Wedgwood design, considered an art form unto itself.

Relief is made by molding the clay with fingers or with the appropriate modeling tools until you obtain your desired effect. The clay application must stick to the walls of a piece without producing any division or cracking during drying and firing. In addition, there should be no significant variations in the thickness of the relief, or imbalance may topple the piece during firing. The clay you use must contain a small amount of nonplastic material, or else the work should be carried out while the clay is still soft.

Paste on Paste

Several thin layers of engobe paste form the basis of this technique, which is also known as *pâte-sur-pâte*. Applied to red bisque clay or fired transparent enamel, the engobe must dry between layers until the desired bas-relief design is formed. Once dried in the open air, it can be smoothed with modeling tools. The engobe is easier to work by adding a thickening agent to it such as gum arabic or tragacanth. Once you have your bas-relief design, coat it with translucent glaze, then fire it. The result will be a lively pattern of lights and shadows as the underlying dark clay is revealed through the relief.

The Chinese first used this technique on porcelain; it was later employed in the West at Sèvres, where it became so popular that it quickly spread throughout Europe. Similar decoration is now made with white paint, which can be dyed with stroke, a watercolorlike underglaze that is also brushed on in fine layers.

▲ **Bas-relief tile.** This clown's head made of red clay takes on an attractive bas-relief that is highlighted with color. M. Paz Vilasaló.

▼ **Applying engobe.** Sketched below, a rubber syringe filled with green engobe is used to apply a leaf pattern in relief on a plate.

▶ **Engobe pattern.** The simple application of engobe stripes adds even more interest to this striking spouted decanter.

Engobes

The simplest ways of applying engobe is by submersion, sprinkling, or spraying. Its application takes practice. Both perseverance and caution must be exercised to prevent water of the liquidy engobe from penetrating the piece. If it does, warping will result, a condition that is difficult to correct. As for color, the engobes suggested for some techniques are toned to contrast with the surface color of the piece. Note that sometimes a ceramic piece must be moistened first for the engobe to adhere to it.

The tools employed for applying engobe vary according to technique. The traditional ox horn, dropper, or syringe are ideal for applying lines and dots. Skill and a steady hand are essential for carrying out this task. The nozzle tip should remain in contact with the piece, and the engobe must be of uniform consistency to flow easily.

The nozzle can also be used for dripping and mottling. The first technique, as its name suggests, simply consists of making droplets by pumping the rubber syringe while moving the nozzle back and forth, up and down, producing an attractive, often unpredictable, look. Mottling is the term for immersing a piece in engobe, then, when it has dried, applying droplets of a different-colored engobe, which are then blended with pen, brush, or comb to create a mottled appearance.

Combing the engobe is another way of producing imaginative patterns. Or if oxygenated water is added to engobe, droplets branch out in the form of lace. Similarly, oil, soluble glaze, soap, and other substances can be added to create a range of original finishes limited only by the artist's imagination in working with them.

Practice and skill are needed to keep the flow uniform when you are applying engobe. Consistency is particularly important when detailed, naturalistic drawings are used rather than abstract shapes or geometric patterns.

Incising

Pointed metal tools can be used to decorate bisque-fired clay, but implements made of wood or bamboo, such as those used by potters in the Far East, are recommended for decorating raw (unfired) clay with shallow or deep grooves. While etching usually refers to designs cut into metal, the word is sometimes used, along with incising, when discussing designs cut into ceramic. The tools employed are the same in either case, but some ceramists think of the lines that are fluid and shallow as incising, and the deeper grooves as etching.

The glaze applied over incising is of vital importance. Some glazes cover the entire pattern, all recessed and raised parts, because they are highly concentrated; more fluid glazes may skip over parts of the surface. An intermediate glaze is the best choice and will produce appealing tones with the subtlest of variations.

▲ Incisions. A fragment of a pre-Columbian vessel reveals a lightly incised linear pattern.

Stamping

Stamping is one of the oldest ways of decorating raw clay without its cracking later. Two imprinting tools are used: stamping wedges, pressed directly into the clay; and cylindrical dies, which are rolled over the clay. In addition to these traditional implements, countless items can be pressed into service (literally) for stamping—buttons, decorative hardware, cookie molds, to name a few; and don't forget tools provided by nature—bark, shells, pine cones.

Tools made of porous materials such as clay and plaster produce a clean stamp; non-porous materials, such as metals, don't give as clean an impression and very often stick to the clay. To prevent this from happening, apply talcum powder to the area that is to be stamped, or lightly oil the roller or wedge.

▼ Stamping. This illustration demonstrates imprinting on wet clay with a wedge stamp.

▶
Incisions. Free-flowing lines incised in raw clay, then highlighted with gold, enhance this contemporary piece. Workshop Group VI.

51

Inlaying

When an incised pattern is filled in, it is called inlaying. The filler is slip or engobe that contrasts in color with that of the underlying bisque body. When it becomes leather-hard (a stage in the drying process of clay when most drying shrinkage has taken place), it is sanded down to the level of the bisque surface. The engobe to be inlaid should not contain any nonplastic materials, such as kaolin, refractory clay, or quartz, as these substances may cause cracks to form.

The inlay technique traces to *Mishima,* a slip-inlay method first practiced by early Korean potters, then adopted and named by the Japanese. The technique became popular during the Middle Ages, especially in the floor-tile industry. Inlaying is incomparable for the precision of design and evenness of surface that can be achieved by skilled artisans. Nonetheless, cracks can form in inlaid clay after it has dried, but this defect can be avoided if the engobe used is carefully selected, as noted above.

Inlaying with a Die

This technique is classified as inlaying, even though clay is not gouged out of the surface to be inlaid. Instead, strips of a contrasting colored clay are superimposed on the soft-clay ground to be adorned, then a die is rolled over the two. One must be careful that pressure on the roller doesn't deform the clay base; changing the tool's direction as needed will prevent this. Very handsome geometric patterns can be made with die inlaying, although they will never be as precise as real inlay.

▶ **Inlay, step 1.**
First the pattern is drawn with slip, then the design is gone over with a gouge.

▶ **Inlay, step 2.**
Incisions are filled with a contrasting engobe.

▼ **Inlay, step 4.**
A transparent glaze heightens the contrast of the two colors.

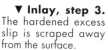

▼ **Inlay, step 3.**
The hardened excess slip is scraped away from the surface.

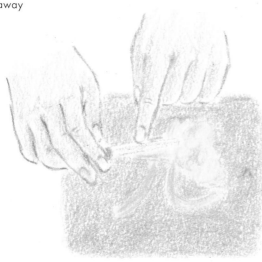

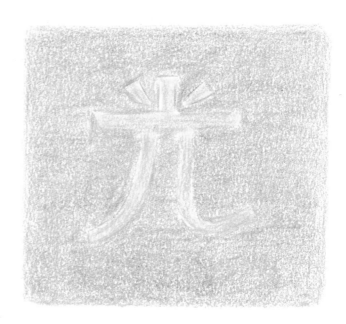

Lithophane

Porcelain impressed with figures that are made distinct by transmitted light is called *lithophane*. Since this process is long and laborious and usually undertaken only by professionals, the brief description here is meant for general information, not instruction.

Several thicknesses of engobe are layered onto porcelain in a particular way that produces varying degrees of translucency, creating the look of a painting when held up to light.

To obtain a transfer print, the motif is designed on a piece of wax of the same thickness as the finished porcelain piece. The transparency of the work can be controlled by examining the wax in front of a light. Once it has been completed, the relief incised in the wax is placed in a plaster mold, from which the porcelain piece is cast. It will have the same thickness and transparency of the wax model.

Faceting

Facets, also called chamfers, are angles other than right angles modeled into ceramics. Faceting is most often used to change the shape of a round pot by shaving the walls to create a multi-sided form. The technique works best on wares with thick walls. When a facet occurs at an edge, it's commonly known as a bevel.

Depending on the consistency of the clay, a cutting wire or a simple knife may be used to make facets, which usually are cut on pieces that have been thrown rather than hand-built. A cutting wire can be used to form facets before removing the piece from the wheel, while the clay is still soft. The clay must harden somewhat before any other tool is used, such as a sharp knife or an implement similar to a potato peeler or cheese slicer.

Facets on a given piece may be uniform in angle, width, and height, or quite varied and irregular for a more abstract look.

▲ **Faceting.** Regularly spaced facets shape this vase.

◄ **Faceting.** Sketch of cutting pattern.

▼ **Lithophane.** Negative and positive photographs of a nineteenth-century porcelain. Museum of Decorative Art, Prague.

Openwork

Openwork is any form of decoration pierced through from one side of an object to the other. Since openings reduce the functionality of a piece, they are normally reserved for ceramics of a purely decorative nature, although fruit bowls are often designed with openwork specifically because it permits air circulation, which keeps fruit fresher.

Openwork is made on half-dry clay with a cutting tool. Once the piece is dry, it is burnished with a damp sponge. In today's ceramics industry, openwork is cut by laser, and the ancient stencil has been replaced by computer.

Piercing can be done with any object that has a sharp, pointed tip: a knife, needle, awl, or square or cylindrical-shaped drill bits or bores that are specially designed for cutting out small sections of clay.

With free rein given to the ceramist's imagination, numerous styles of openwork can be devised—from punched holes in a simple repeat pattern, to intricate latticework, to bold, abstract cutouts.

▲ Openwork. Openwork cut in raw clay is highlighted by relief outline in this lamp base. Montserrat Roura.

◄ Openwork. The free-form cutouts of this contemporary vase were created before bisque-firing. M. Pilar Navarro.

Lacework

Porcelain lacework (common in period-costumed figurines) is made by dipping cotton lace in engobe that has glue added to it. Frequently, the engobe fills many of the openings in the lacework pattern. The holes must then be cleaned out with a needle one by one, a task that requires a great deal of patience.

During firing, the cotton lace actually burns, leaving only an imprint produced on the engobe. This type of lacework is extremely fragile and should be glazed with caution, since it will break under the slightest pressure. Glaze firing reinforces it, but it is still delicate. Ceramic lacework can be made only with cotton; other materials, such as nylon, melt and disintegrate at high kiln temperatures, before the slip has a chance to solidify.

Sgraffito

Related to incising and executed with the same tools, *sgraffito,* the Italian word for "scratched," is the technique of scraping through one layer of slip or glaze to reveal another underneath of contrasting color. Exquisite designs can be created with this method, especially when the surface has been layered with several slips or glazes of different colors.

The contrasts between the colors that emerge below the incised lines make this technique distinctive, so even though sgraffito produces a relief, it is the color that embellishes and distinguishes it.

The surface of an incised area must be kept soft and smooth. For best results, it's preferable to use wooden modeling tools, because metal instruments leave marks that are difficult to remove.

When you apply sgraffito to a glazed bisque clay piece, start as soon as it is dry. If you wait too long, the glaze will begin to peel and the lines will be unstable. The surface of unfired clay is very different from the hard surface of a bisque-fired piece, and the scratching technique must be adjusted accordingly.

Etching

Although the term is usually associated with metal, etching on ceramics is a similar process: making a design by means of the action of hydrofluoric acid eating away at parts of a surface to expose other parts beneath.

It is a difficult and laborious technique, normally employed only in the decoration of high-quality porcelain pieces. There are a few ways to obtain the same effect: etching by hand, sprinkling, or using an insulating glaze. The easiest method for a beginner is etching by hand.

On a glaze-coated ground, a pattern is drawn using a brush or fountain pen loaded with liquid asphalt thinned slightly with turpentine. This protects the design from the corrosive effects of the acid bath that follows. *Protective gloves must be worn throughout the entire process to avoid burning the skin.*

The acid is placed in a plastic tub (preferably made of polyethylene) and the piece is submerged until the acid has eaten away about a millimeter (less than a sixteenth of an inch) of the exposed glaze. The longer the ware remains in acid, the greater the depth of erosion. Immediately after removing the piece from the acid bath, it is washed with abundant water first and then with turpentine to remove the asphalt. The corrosive action of the acid will have eaten away the unprotected parts of the coated porcelain. The finish appears dull in the etched parts, in contrast to the lustrous parts of the original glaze.

Decals, gold serigraphs, thermoplastic serigraphs, and certain etching glazes can also be considered forms of etching pottery, but these techniques are most often employed in decorations that use only gold as color.

▲ Etched plate.
The contrast between the dull and shiny areas of this porcelain plate reveals how acid affects surface finish in the etching process. M. Pilar Navarro.

◄ Sgraffito.
Engobe was first added to this jar, then the figural depiction of the Saint George legend was scraped into it. M. Pilar Navarro.

Decorating with Paint

The word *paint* in this context encompasses colorants, glazes, gold, pencils, colored slips, and other mediums discussed in this section. All may be applied over bisque, the term for the fired, unglazed clay object that you wish to decorate.

Reserves

This technique leaves part of the bisque free of color or prevents a different color from invading it. There are several ways to achieve this look.

Masks

A mask is a cut-out pattern (positive or negative) that is placed on the ceramic object; then, with a sponge or cloth pad, paint is applied within and/or around it. Akin to templates, masks can produce a hand-painted look without requiring the decorator to do creative drawing or careful brushwork.

The first masks were metallic and came in various thicknesses. Now they are made of a treated, waterproof paper and may be simple shapes that the decorator uses individually or combines with other shapes to create more complex designs.

Wax

Wax resist is a decorative technique based on application of a pattern of hot or cold liquid wax to selected areas of a ceramic piece. When the wax hardens, glaze, slip, or other colorants applied to the piece will adhere only to the unwaxed areas. Wax will bond to either raw or bisque-fired clay; it melts away during firing.

Hot wax is not recommended for beginners, since its temperature must be constantly regulated very precisely to get good results. Cold-wax emul-

sion, on the other hand, doesn't require temperature control, doesn't have the characteristic bad smell of hot wax, and there is no fire risk involved. Just ensure that the layer of wax emulsion that you brush on is not too thin, and don't touch the piece until the wax has dried completely. (Wax takes longer to dry on leatherhard clay. On bisque ware or over raw glaze, it takes under a half hour.) And always wash brushes thoroughly immediately after each use.

Wax brushed on leatherhard clay is an alternative base for sgraffito decoration (which is usually scratched through a slip or glaze coating).

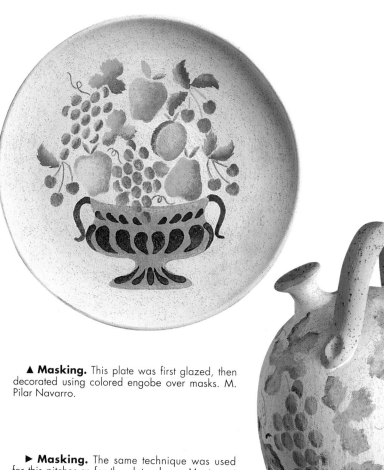

▲ **Masking.** This plate was first glazed, then decorated using colored engobe over masks. M. Pilar Navarro.

▶ **Masking.** The same technique was used for this pitcher as for the plate above. Montserrat Roura.

◀ **Wax resist.** The raw bisque areas of this free-form pattern is where wax was applied. When green glaze was added, it resisted all waxed areas, producing this handsome contemporary look. Workshop Group VI.

Liquid Latex

Bought in paste form, then thinned with water, latex can be used instead of wax to accomplish the same reserve effect (but sgraffito can never be done on latex). It forms a film that can be easily peeled off, must be removed before firing, and is generally applied to bisque or unglazed clay.

Your brush should be soaked in water before dipping it into latex, and take care not to let latex harden on the bristles, or the brush will be ruined.

Since latex peels off easily, it's possible to correct mistakes or change patterns before applying glaze. Note, however, that latex doesn't always adhere well during the painting process. Also, in contrast to other materials reviewed here, this one is very new to ceramics decoration. Therefore, its effects and potential haven't yet been fully tested.

Adhesive Tapes

While they don't stick very well to bisque clay, tapes work fine on glazed surfaces that have been fired, and are useful for making straight lines. Cloth, plastic, and paper tapes are available, although with some types, there is the danger that paint may ooze underneath the edges, producing uneven lines. If that happens, try to turn it into an advantage. Uneven lines often appear to have been drawn freehand—a sophisticated design element.

In addition to rolls of tape, self-stick papers that come in sheets or rolls, often with plasticized finishes, can be cut into desired shapes.

◄ **Tapes.** Both tapes and cutouts from self-stick paper were used to create stripes and geometric patterns on this jar. M. Pilar Navarro.

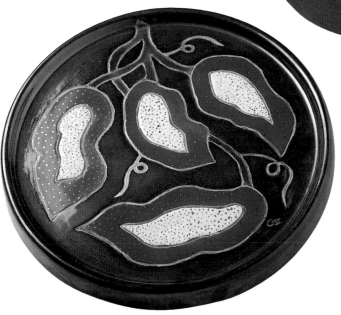

◄ **Latex.** A stylized leaf pattern was covered with latex, so that when brown glaze was applied, it adhered only to the plate's background. When the latex was peeled off, the leaves and stems were then painted with their several glazes. Workshop Group VI.

► **Self-stick papers.** Cutouts from plasticized, self-stick papers created the flowing shapes on this square vase. Workshop Group VI.

Cuerda Seca

To keep glazes of different colors from meeting and mixing on a ceramic surface, a thin line is drawn to separate them. Known as *cuerda seca* ("dry line"), this division is traditionally made with a grease and manganese mixture, but the simplest way to achieve the effect is to draw the line with an underglaze.

In medieval times, cuerda seca was painted with dyed wax. A fine example of this technique can be seen in exquisite Hispano-Moorish tiles of the period. Oil paints have also been used as cuerda seca reserve.

In porcelain decoration, a paint mixed from powdered sugar, pigment, and water is used to separate colors. Drawn with a pen, the line stops colors from merging, acting as a cuerda seca.

▲ **Cuerda seca.** The clean division of colors in the symmetrical pattern on this round plaque was achieved by placing lines between colors. Gold was then added to accentuate the lines. M. Pilar Navarro.

▶ **Cuerda seca.** An underglaze was employed as a cuerda seca to separate the glazes on this tall, cylindrical vase. M. Pilar Navarro.

▼ **Cuerda seca.** Subtle colors are separated on this porcelain tray by a preparation of sugar, water, and pigment. M. Pilar Navarro.

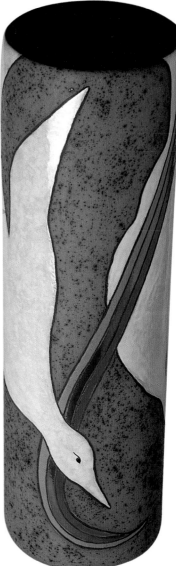

Dabbers or Sponges

Equally efficient for applying color on bisque or glazed clay, sponges and cloth dabbers on handles have been used for centuries to produce uniform or specially textured finishes. It's helpful to add drops of essence of clove to the glaze first to slow down its drying time, thereby giving you a longer period to work with the sponge or dabber.

Of the many qualities of sponges on the market, natural ones are the best, although any kind can be used if its contours and crevices produce a texture you like. Or perhaps you want an absence of texture—a uniform consistency of glaze that's sometimes easier to obtain by sponge or dabber than it is by brush.

The same can be said for dabbers. The texture of the cloth will leave its mark on paint applications. So for the smoothest look, as when working on porcelain, a dabber made of natural silk should be employed. It will not leave texture marks on paint applied atop fired glaze.

▶ **Sponge.** The gently curved sections of subtle color that make up the decoration on this vase were done with many successive, sponge-soaked applications of three tones of glaze. To give the vase an even more luminous finish, an extra pearl-like layer was added. M. Pilar Navarro.

▲ **Sponge and dabber tools.** Sketches show how a sponge (top) and dabber (below) can be given wooden handles to facilitate use.

▶ **Sponge types.** Different sizes, textures, and contours of sponges offer a wide range of decorating options.

Pastels and Colored Pencils

Ordinary colored pencils and pastels can be used to draw finished designs on ceramics. Just as with paint or other mediums, they are applied to bisque that is then fired. Pastels and colored pencils are easy to use and are especially well suited to creating delicate designs.

Instead of buying pastels, very ambitious artisans might try making their own. Mix a solution of about an ounce (twenty-eight grams) of gum arabic (gum tragacanth, gelatin, or casein may be used instead) with a little over a quart (one liter) of water—the concentration depends on how hard you want the pastels to be—then add white clay or kaolin in powder form. Once the paste is ready, form it into sticks by rolling it in gummed paper. Allow the sticks to dry, then peel the paper down a bit to expose working ends.

When pastels are used to decorate unfired glaze, excess dust is removed by blowing gently over the surface. If you don't do so, it will merge with the glaze during firing.

▼ **Colored pencils.** Sharp-pointed colored pencils produced the delicate floral bouquet on this small plate. Notice how the rim zigzag pattern is coordinated to the central motif. M. Pilar Navarro.

60

Stencils

One variety of stencil has the design perforated with pinholes on a sheet of paper, which is placed on the ceramic piece. A pad coated with graphite powder (scraped from a soft-lead pencil) is then pressed lightly through the perforations to outline the drawing on the ware. Special carbon-transfer paper may also be used for tracings.

► **Transfer carbon.** Carbon papers for transferring designs to bisque surfaces come in various colors.

► **Traced design.** A porcelain plate's design was traced down, but some of the leaves in shadow and the entire rim of the plate were painted directly with overglazes.

▼ **Stencil.** The sketch below at left shows a dabber coated with graphite powder being run over a perforated stencil to impress the design on a ceramic surface. The sketch below at right shows the perforated design, a long-tailed bird, drawn to follow the round contour of a plate.

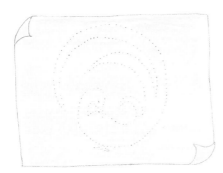

Rubber Stamps

Rubber stamps are first impregnated with paint, then pressed on a ceramic surface either under or over fired glaze. If precious metal pigments are used, a few drops of essence of clove should be added.

Ceramists often make their own stamp designs. It's a three-step process: First, the pattern is carved out of wood or plaster; then a clay or plaster mold is made; then the rubber stamp is cast from the mold. The stamp is attached to a wooden handle, with a piece of sponge inserted between it and the handle to give the tool flexibility for printing on curved surfaces.

Use only alcohol to clean stamps, since it will not damage the rubber.

▼ **Rubber stamp.** A ceramic mug is imprinted by rubber stamp.

Decals

Decals on specially treated, kiln-proof paper come in a wide array of designs. To transfer the design to glazed pottery, wet the decal with water, fasten it to the piece, then smooth with a sponge to remove excess dampness and air bubbles.

Normally applied to glazed and fired pieces, decals can produce beautiful and high-quality designs with sharp details, but they can't be compared to fine, hand-painted creations.

61

Screen Printing

Serigraphy, the printmaking process based on stenciling, was adapted to ceramics by Chinese and Japanese potters centuries ago. Their stencil was a canvas of woven hair over which, on the reverse side, cutout paper drawings were placed. Nowadays, pure silk or synthetic fabrics are used, stretched taut over a wood or metal frame, with masks used to produce the design. The printing medium is pushed through open areas of the screen mesh with a squeegee and deposited in a thin layer on the ceramic surface. Underglazes and glaze paints are mediums used in this technique.

To sharpen the print, serigraphic impression oil can be added. Both it and ready-made colors for ceramics screen printing are carried by many crafts dealers.

Underglaze Paints

These colors are used to decorate white and red clay objects that are either raw or bisque-fired; available in solid or semiliquid form, the paints are applied before the final transparent enamel coating is added.

Underglazes may be fired at temperatures of about 1900–2500 degrees Fahrenheit (900–1200 degrees centigrade). The painted parts have to maintain the same amount of porosity as the bisque clay for the glaze to produce a uniform effect over the entire piece.

Underglazes are generally mixed with water or turpentine, but if the dilution is oily, the clay object should be fired before glazing; otherwise the glaze will run.

▲ **Underglazes.** Oriental decoration on white bisque clay, later covered with transparent glaze, is highlighted with gold details. M. Pilar Navarro.

◄ **Underglazes.** Tiles depicting different species of birds adorn an exterior wall. The engobed raw clay tiles were underglazed, then finished with a transparent glaze. M. Pilar Navarro.

Glazes and Enamels

The broad range of glazes and enamels sold are classified by the properties of the components from which they are made. They may produce transparent, gloss, matte, opaque, or colored finishes, depending on their specific ingredients. Certain enamels create textured finishes, such as crinkled, spongy, metallic, and other special effects.

Many glazes and enamels can be combined on a single piece, in which case, firing should be at about 2100 degrees Fahrenheit (1000 degrees centigrade), normally with the use of pyrometric cones.

◄ **Multiple glazes.** Successive glazes, spatter technique, and an unusual tear shape make this a striking vase. Montserrat Roura.

▲ **Multiple glazes.** The rainbow of glazes decorating this pair of ornate urns is consistent with the rather overelaborate style that was very common at the beginning of the twentieth century. Private collection.

◄ **Multiple glazes.** Successive glazes give this long-necked vase a brilliant finish. Its golden glow is owed to a glaze—not, as might be thought, from metallic gold. M. Pilar Navarro.

Painting over Raw Glaze

Potters have been applying paint to opaque white glaze for many centuries. Majolica is a prime example of the technique.

The paint employed for this purpose is manufactured with the same pigments as those of underglaze paints, but its melting point must be lower than the latter so that it fuses properly with the glaze during firing. If necessary, the paint can be thinned with water or several drops of glycerin. If stroke paint is used—an underglaze that produces a transparent effect—it must be somewhat thicker than usual in order to be emphatic enough. The ware is fired at about 2000 degrees Fahrenheit (1000 degrees centigrade).

Overglaze Techniques

Two groups of very different techniques fit into this category. One employs paints similar to those used for underglazing but with a lower melting point, the colors fusing themselves onto the original glaze during firing; the other includes metallic overglazes, such as gold, silver, and lusters that form only a very fine film over the glaze, which wears away with time.

◀ **Paint over raw glaze.** A glassy finish is produced by paint on raw glaze on this plate depicting a village rendered in a charming, naive style.

◀ **Overglaze.** Decoration on white porcelain features birds highlighted on a white background with a surrounding strip of red interrupted by butterfly medallions. M. Pilar Navarro.

▼ **Metallic overglaze.** The liberal use of gold against dark, variegated tones gives this egg-shaped piece its luxurious sheen. M. Pilar Navarro.

▼ **Paint over raw glaze.** Light brushstrokes are outlined here and there to heighten a delicate floral painted in a loose, spontaneous style on this shallow box. M. Pilar Navarro.

Painting on Porcelain

This technique differs somewhat from other methods described up to this point. While this type of decoration can be applied to earthenware or other types of glazed ceramics, it's most successful on porcelain. The colors come in fine powder form and are mixed with an oil medium, normally using a spatula on a glass tile, until a creamy consistency is obtained that makes the paints easy to apply by brush. You can also buy water-based colors or watercolor cakes, which are known as "third-firing" colors.

The oils used as diluents are volatile substances that evaporate during firing and leave a highly adhesive resinous sediment. These oil mediums may be vegetable or mineral in origin. There are many kinds available that are appropriate for this work, some of which can even be mixed together to obtain the best consistency. It's important that the oil medium not dry too quickly so that a half-painted piece may be left standing for several days before being completed.

The viscosity of the oil must also be taken into account, according to the technique you are using. If you're working with a nib or applying backgrounds, the pigment has to be diluted with more oil than usual.

For most applications, a suitable mix should consist of nine parts white mineral oil with one part copaiba oil. But the choice of oil offers many options; it's a matter of testing until you find one that meets your needs.

Although painting on porcelain is usually done with a brush, surfaces can also be covered by immersion, with a sponge or pad, spraying, or dusting. Porcelain firing is at done at about 1600 degrees Fahrenheit (750 degrees centigrade).

▲ **Porcelain.** Inspired by a motif on an eighteenth-century European plate, this landscape includes some subtle gold accents. M. Pilar Navarro.

▼ **Porcelain.** Painting on porcelain using a stumping technique—shading and blending usually associated with pastel or charcoal drawing—makes it possible to obtain chiaroscuro effects that highlight the design, making gold unnecessary in this case. Sofía Ciro.

Gold and Silver

Both metals are sold in liquid form, and certain brands are precolored to make application easier, since some glazes with which they may be combined will not show tints emphatically. There is also a product available, although it is somewhat more expensive, called matte gold, also known as Roman gold, which can be bought in liquid or tablet form and dissolved in commercial solvent or lavender oil. *But take care not to dilute it too much.* It is almost impossible to predict exact proportions. Experimenting with different amounts will lead you to the appropriate consistency for your application.

The degree of brilliance of gold or silver depends on the glaze over which it has been applied; over matte, it's duller than over a shiny glaze, which will highlight it.

Matte gold has to be burnished to become shiny, using polishing sand, a special fiberglass broom, or agate stone. *Extreme care* should be taken to avoid touching the gold with your fingers before polishing it; otherwise, fingerprints will prove impossible to remove, even by polishing. The only solution to this predicament is to refire the piece.

Shiny gold in liquid form is the most common material used, not only because it's the most economical, but also because it's the easiest to apply. Small touches of gold, delicate little arabesque flourishes, or a simple line around the edge of the plate are applied to highlight a piece in many designs. It's important that your work space be perfectly clean, dust-free, and well ventilated; your hands should also be clean, free of grease, and completely dry.

The piece to be decorated should be cleaned with a cloth dampened with alcohol, or, if that's not handy, saliva—*not water*—should be substituted. If you do make a mistake or apply gold to an unintended area, wet a corner of the cloth with your tongue and wipe it over the stain; *never* do it with water or turpentine, or you will have a major disaster on your hands. Only saliva can be substituted for alcohol, or perhaps we should say that only alcohol can replace saliva, which is the most effective liquid for removal of gold from porcelain.

Gold or silver should be painted with a soft-bristle brush, the size determined by the area you are working on and the detailing required. Reserve the brush for this use only. Lines should be of uniform thickness, but not so thick as to create a relief. Check to see that the tone is uniform over the entire surface once the

▲ Gold filigree. Delicate gold work was applied to this porcelain plate with a pen nib. M. Pilar Navarro.

▶ Gold over glaze. Ruby glaze shows through the gold applied with a sponge on these companion pieces. M. Pilar Navarro.

metallic glaze has been completely applied.

When the brush is cleaned in a jar containing alcohol, the gold falls from the bristles and settles on the bottom of the container, so that it can be retrieved once the alcohol has evaporated. I personally do not clean the brushes I use for gold and silver, preferring instead to let the gold dry on the bristles, and when I need to use that brush again, the new gold softens the remaining sediment, rescuing the precious product for my next project.

There are several implements made specifically for continuous line applications, but I prefer to work with a brush, which is not only efficient for continuous line work, but for all manner of designs and embellishments without having to change tools.

I often use my fingertip to paint the border of a plate—the index finger tends to work best. I dip my finger in gold and let it brush the edge as I turn the plate with my other hand. For a thicker line, I simply apply more pressure to the piece.

If you prefer, a small natural sponge can be used in the same way as your finger. If you're going to use the sponge more than once, it should be kept in an airtight container. When it becomes saturated with gold, it can still be used by soaking it in turpentine and then washing it with detergent. This procedure will leave the sponge like new, but note that you will lose the gold that gets tossed out with the turpentine.

▲ **Silver decoration.** Fired dark glaze is an effective background for this graceful silver pattern. Workshop Group VI.

▼ **Gold decoration.** Overglazed flowers and gold embellishments are characteristic of fine Limoges ware. M. Pilar Navarro.

Lusters

Lusters have been in use for more than a millennium, and some exquisite examples of early work employing these colors can be seen to this day.

Luster colors are manufactured by melting a resin with metallic hydrates, then suspending the precipitate in oil of lavender or rosemary. Lusters come in blue (cobalt), green (chrome), pink (bismuth-gold), or they can be colorless (bismuth, lead, zinc). They should be applied to areas of the piece that are free of dust and fingerprints, using a brush, spray, or simply fingers. Since luster dries quickly, it's important to work lightly in thin layers. If it is applied thickly, there is danger of its peeling during firing. After applying luster, the piece should be left in a dust-free, draft-free room to dry. Once it has dried, however, dust will not stick to it.

After cleaning your brushes with universal solvent, dry them by squeezing the bristles with a cloth, then wash them several times with small amounts of alcohol until all the luster is removed. When you're sure no luster remains, let your brushes dry, then blow through the bristles so that they remain loose and soft. *Never use turpentine to wash these brushes,* and have one brush for each luster to avoid mixing colors.

Luster is fired at a temperature that is lower than the melting point of the base glaze, but it needs good ventilation; thus, pieces to which luster has been applied should not be placed too close together in the kiln so as to ensure adequate air circulation between them. Several lusters can be put on a single piece, but the object must be fired between applications.

Decorating an object can be a complex procedure because so many factors are at play that might alter the result. The techniques we've reviewed may be combined, an excellent way to build up your experience. Other basic ingredients for obtaining good results are practice, boldness, patience, and imagination.

▼ **Mother-of-pearl luster.** Relief work and a pearly finish highlight this oval box. M. Pilar Navarro.

▶ **Pink luster.** The beauty of this traditionally shaped vase is enhanced by its lustrous finish. Workshop Group VI.

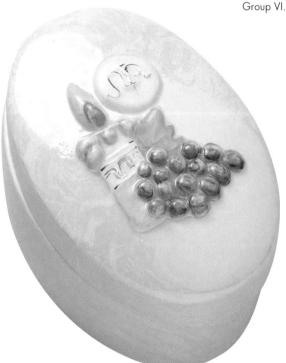

► **Luster and gold.** This coffee service combines luster and gold, a very fashionable Art Deco style during the 1920s.

PRACTICING
CERAMICS DECORATION

This section will demonstrate many of the techniques reviewed in our opening chapter on the history of ceramics decoration. To make each procedure as clear and easy to follow as possible, all instructions are in step-by-step format and fully illustrated.

Fourteen separate decorating projects are featured in this chapter, each based on a different technique to start you off with a firm footing and broad range of choices. Once you've practiced them individually, you'll be prepared to start combining techniques, experimenting to find your own new forms of decoration, which is one of the great pleasures of this craft.

We hope that you will see the examples in this chapter primarily as learning guides that will soon launch you into the exciting experience of creating your own original designs for personal and gift use.

Selecting a Piece and Decoration Method for It

Before embarking on a project, you should have a clear idea of what you want to make. Will it be given as a gift? Must it be functional, or just decorative? Will it be used only on special occasions? What technique are you going to choose?

By clearly defining your objectives, you will quickly establish which ceramic object to shop for, which materials you'll need to embellish it, which colors to choose, and how to conceive and lay out your design.

If the piece is for yourself, the most important consideration will be personal taste—in which case, just allow your intuition to guide all your decisions. But if your creation is destined for a friend, *that* person's taste, not yours, should certainly be the decisive factor. For instance, someone equipped with the latest hi-tech kitchen is unlikely to appreciate a rococo teapot decorated with gold. Family and friends will be doubly grateful for a present that's custom designed to the recipient's taste and setting.

If creating a strictly decorative object is your aim, your focus will be on its beauty, affording you great freedom of choice with materials and design. However, if the piece is to be functional, you must consider how it will be used and those design restrictions that may be imposed by such usage. For example, dinner service and other objects designed to hold food *must be glazed with nontoxic products (no lead content)*. Likewise, vases, pitchers, or any other piece that will hold liquid *must be glazed on the inside as well as outside*.

Each project is unique, and the result is different each time—even when two people apply the same decoration to two identical pieces. Everything—from the particular hand with which an underglaze is applied, to the place in which the piece is packed in the kiln for firing—contributes to making each decorating experience a singular one.

◀ **Studio shelves.** Building up an inventory of pigments, glazes, and other decorating materials will broaden your options in making design choices.

▼ **Studio worktable.** Even though it may appear chaotic, this is what an active decorator's studio looks like most of the time.

Preparing to Decorate Bisque-Fired Objects

Perhaps you already have some experience in decorating ceramics. But even if that's so, this should be a useful refresher course in the steps to take before embarking on the embellishment of a piece, from the time you buy it to the moment you remove it from the kiln.

We recommend that beginners start with a flat-surfaced object, since the more uneven the surface, the more difficult it will be to decorate.

With this first and all other decorating projects, always heed the following instructions before you begin.

► **1.** The piece must be burnished with fine-grained sandpaper until it is smooth.

◄ **2.** After blowing away any remaining dust, go over the surface with a clean brush.

◄ 3. Wipe the surface well with a damp sponge.

▼ 4. Once the object is dry, draw your motif with a soft lead pencil.

If you're not ready to make an original drawing, trace a design you think would be attractive for the piece. Don't be embarrassed about tracing—many potters do it. Your focus is on decorating ceramics, not on studying drawing. Trace over design transfer paper; the lines will disappear on firing.

Once your design is all traced down, you're ready to decorate with your chosen technique.

Underglazing Techniques:
Decorating a Plate with Simple Motifs

By underglazing we mean those techniques in which color is applied directly to the bisque (fired, unglazed clay), then covered with transparent glaze at the end of the process.

The drawing chosen for this exercise is quite simple: a crisp, clean winter holly motif that can be used to create an ideal seasonal gift.

Materials
- White bisque plate.
- Brushes: #4 round, #4 or 6 bright, #00 outline, and #14 or 16 wide flat for glazing. (As noted earlier in the materials section, "brights" are modified flat brushes.)

- Paints: stroke, or translucent underglazes (light green, dark green, yellow, and dark yellow or orange; some brands also come in red). Clear transparent glaze for final coat.
- Miscellaneous: rags, jar to hold water.

◄ **1.** My drawing is made with colored pencils; the colors are fairly close in value (relative lightness and darkness) to the paints I will use on the plate.

◄ **2.** To prepare the plate, I follow the four general rules given on the preceding two pages.

▼ **3.** I usually copy my drawing (rather than trace it) directly onto the plate, using lead pencil, which won't smear when it's painted over.

▲ **4.** Painting the leaves first with three coats of light green, I allow each coat to dry before proceeding with the next. Once the third coat is dry, I start painting the veins and outlining the leaves in dark green. One layer should be enough there.

◄ **5.** The plate's border is also painted in dark green. This requires three layers, with drying time between each.

▶ **6.** I dip a #4 or 6 bright brush into yellow and paint the ribbon streamers and loops, in one gesture for each if possible.

◀ **7.** Two more coats of yellow are applied, then dark yellow or orange to make the ribbon stand out a bit more.

◄ **8.** Finally, I paint the holly berries with three layers of red, making sure that the previous coat is dry before going to the next.

► **9.** The thin twigs attached to the berries and leaves are painted in dark green, using the #00 outline brush.

For this plate to have a perfect finish, at this point, fire it at a cone 04 temperature. However, if no kiln is available at this step, it won't matter; the effect would be so subtle that you probably wouldn't discern the difference. Usually the reason a piece is fired before glazing is to rectify any areas that are not entirely covered in paint.

▲ 10. Once the paint is totally dry, I apply clear glaze with a #14 or 16 flat brush. (Note that before firing, some brands of glaze have a light tone, but they all turn transparent after firing.) Two layers of glaze must be used, and again, I emphasize that the first must be totally dry before you can apply the second. (When the tone has turned lighter, the first layer is dry.) The time a glaze takes to dry depends on the surface to which it is applied; generally, it takes no more than half an hour.

▲ 11. For ease of handling and placement in the kiln, leave the underside of the plate unglazed, since this is the part that will rest on the oven shelf.

▶ 12. Here is the plate after it has been fired. If you wish, you can add your signature to your work, or initials, as I did with mine (near the-bottom berries) before the firing.

Now that you've tried your first piece and are proud of your effort, you are probably eager to start on another creation.

◄ **Sketch.** While the colors in this drawing differ somewhat from the finished plate, the values are close enough to project how they will look when translated into paint.

▼ **Underglaze.** The same technique is used as in the previous example, but this fuller design presents more challenging detail work.

Decorating a Vase with Opaque Underglazes: Relief Designs

This technique differs from the previous one in that it uses opaque (rather than translucent) underglaze, which acts like slip to produce a relief effect. Final glaze is then added. Certain products for relief make the final glaze unnecessary, although I find it advisable to apply at least one coat. Optional interior glaze is discussed at the end of this demonstration, so read the instructions through before starting, as interior glazing must be done first if you want to waterproof your vase for holding fresh flowers.

Materials
- Red or white bisque vase.
- Brushes: flats; #2, 4, and/or 6 rounds.
- Fine-grain sponge for applying background glaze.
- Paint: opaque underglaze of color chosen for background.
- Cream-colored engobe for relief work.
- Transparent glaze.

◄ **1.** I sketch my pattern, using color in the negative space to show how that background shade will look with a cream-colored floral against it.

▼ **3.** Using a sponge loaded with paint (opaque underglaze or slip) chosen for the background, I cover the vase body with three layers (if painting on red clay, make it four), allowing each to dry before going on to the next.

◄ **2.** As always, I begin by burnishing the surface of the piece with sandpaper, then wiping off the dust very thoroughly.

◄ **4.** After the final layer has dried, I draw or trace down my floral design, which I plan to fill in with the natural-colored engobe. (If I wanted it colored, it could be glazed later or painted with underglaze stroke.)

▶ **5.** For a thick relief, you should apply at least three or four layers of engobe. The first layer, however, must be diluted with distilled water until it has a creamy consistency; mix it on a glazed tile or similar surface, adding water until you get it flowing. Use a flat or round brush, depending on the size and shape of your drawing. After the first layer has dried, I apply two more, slightly thicker, layers, with drying time between each. If the relief appears somewhat glossy, add another layer, and try to keep your raised design smooth and consistent in depth.

◄ **6.** When my relief design is completed, using a #2 flat brush dipped in clear glaze, first I put a strip of glaze around the design, following its contours carefully, then I load the brush with glaze and apply a layer over the rest of the surface, covering all the background color.

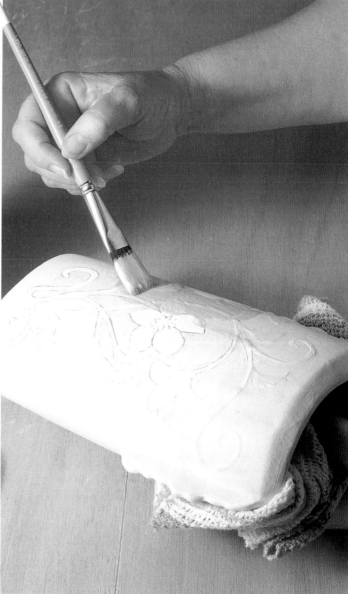

► **7.** When the glaze is dry, I apply a second coat, this time also covering the relief. The vase is now ready to be fired at a cone 06 temperature.

▼ 8. After firing, another optional step may be added to highlight the decoration: an outline of the relief with a line of gold, silver, or platinum underglaze, which is then refired.

Detail. This close-up section of the vase (below, left) shows the work more clearly, with a fine line of silver glaze added around the design.

Waterproofed vase. If the vase is to hold fresh flowers, the interior must be sealed with glaze to make it waterproof, a step that is best taken before any exterior decoration is applied.

Dilute enough glaze with water to cover the entire inner surface of the vase—the proportion is about nine parts glaze to one part water. Pour in and spread the glaze by rolling the vase slowly around, or if the vase opening is wide enough, use a flat brush to spread it. If you use too much glaze, just pour out the excess.

If you coat the inside after your exterior decoration is completed, you must be extra careful not to stain your surface design. If this should happen, let it dry and remove the stain with sandpaper. But it's best to avoid trouble by getting into the habit of glazing the inside of pieces at the start. Imagine, for instance, if you had used matte glaze or another kind that's incompatible with the interior glaze and, on bathing the inside of the piece with glaze, you accidentally marred the outer surface. It simply doesn't pay to take unnecessary risks.

Decorating an Engobed Tray with Sgraffito

Since this decoration method also requires a final glaze, it can be considered an underglazing technique.

It is not essential to use an engobed piece. You can also choose white kaolin bisque to which three layers of any color slip you wish can be applied. Either engobe or layered slip provides a suitable base on which to scratch out the sgraffito.

Materials
- Small tray with raw engobe (does not have to be sanded).
- Brushes: #6 round, #2 ,4, flat, #16 wide flat for glazing.
- Paints: opaque underglazes (colors according to design); clear transparent glaze for final coat.
- Punch or pointed tool; lancet or kitchen knife.

▲ **1.** My sketch is colored in with crayons to simulate the glaze hues I'll use.

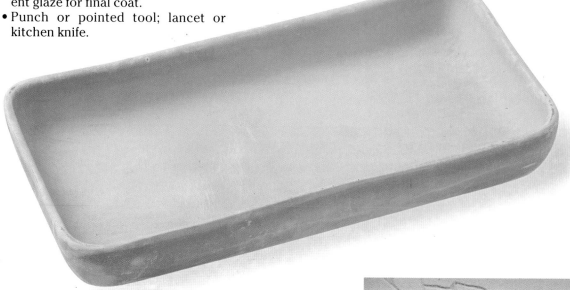

▲ **2.** This is the sanded piece, just as it was purchased, ready for sgraffito incising.

▶ **3.** Here's a detail of the sgraffito made with a punch. When incised, the base color, red clay, will show through the engobe coating a bit.

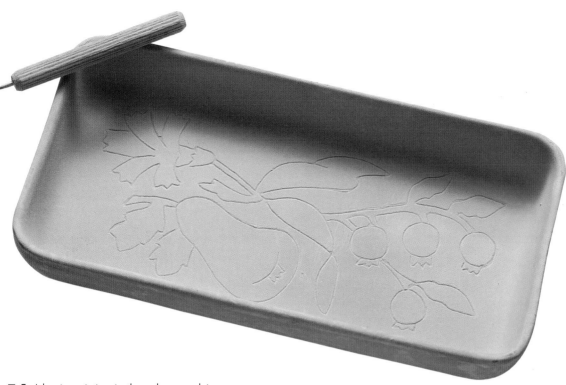

◄ **4.** Sgraffito of the whole design has now been placed on the tray. If the surface seems to need a little more pattern, you can always scratch other lines into it.

▼ **5.** I begin painting in the colors, applying three coats of each. As usual, each layer of color must dry before you add the next.

▲ **6.** As the piece I'm working on is raw, it is advisable to fire it at this point, since the dampness of the overglaze I will apply next might weaken the tray and break it. Notice that I've scraped the tray's rim to expose the raw red clay under the engobed bisque.

▶ **7.** Once the piece has been fired, I apply two layers of glaze, with drying time in between. Finally, I fire it again.

► **8.** This close-up detail of the fired piece shows the color of the red clay in the design's sgraffito-incised outline.

▼ **9.** Notice how, after firing, the colors of the tray are much richer than they appear on the opposite page in their unfired state; they owe much of this effect to the final overglaze applied.

Decorating a Jewel Box with Marbling

As this demonstration will show, an elegant look of simulated marble is easy to produce on clay by simply blowing a few drops of color onto the surface. While the technique is easy, for consistently good results, specific steps should be followed.

Materials
- A jewel box made of white bisque.
- Brushes: #6 flat, #14 wide flat.
- Paints: opaque brown and ivory or cream; strokes (translucent underglazes) of blue, pink, and black.
- Clear transparent glaze.
- Mother-of-pearl luster and appropriate solvent.
- Liquid latex.
- Three droppers: a pipette, tube, straw, or similar item.

◀ **1.** I sand down and clean the piece to prepare it for decorating.

▲ **2.** With pencil, I mark off those parts of the box and lid that are to be marbled.

◀ **3.** The lightest opaque color is painted on first—three coats in all, with drying time between layers.

Using the same color, I apply triple layers (with drying time between) to the inside of both the box base and lid.

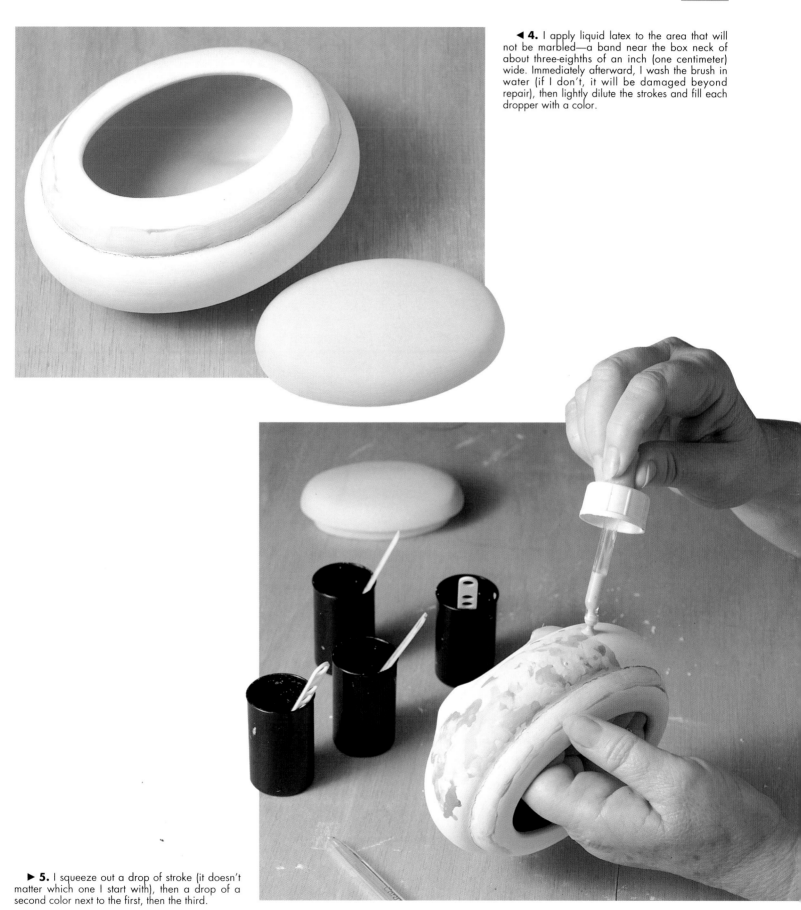

◀ **4.** I apply liquid latex to the area that will not be marbled—a band near the box neck of about three-eighths of an inch (one centimeter) wide. Immediately afterward, I wash the brush in water (if I don't, it will be damaged beyond repair), then lightly dilute the strokes and fill each dropper with a color.

▶ **5.** I squeeze out a drop of stroke (it doesn't matter which one I start with), then a drop of a second color next to the first, then the third.

◄ **6.** Before the drops have had a chance to run, I blow through the tube and force them toward a neighboring color.

By intermixing drops of the three strokes and repeating these steps of squeezing out drops and blowing on them as many times as needed, I gradually obtain a marbled effect.

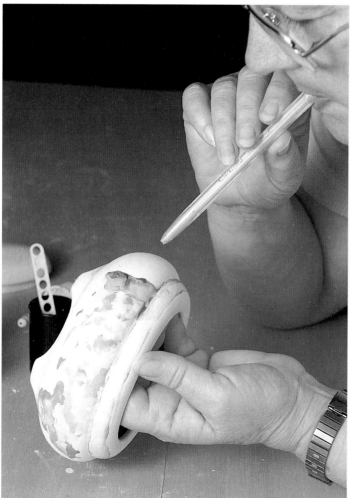

▼ **7.** Once the surface is painted and dried, I remove the latex by raising it with a pointed tool, which should peel it off with relative ease. The box must then be checked thoroughly to be sure there's no remaining latex; I then sand down the exposed neck rim to remove any further residue.

◄ **8.** Now I apply three layers of opaque brown to the neck and feet of the jewel box, of course allowing the respective layers to dry. Although not essential, it's a good idea to fire the piece after this eighth step so that the colors are fixed securely before glazing.

▶ **9.** After firing the piece, I glaze the inside and outside of both the box and lid, using a wide brush saturated with clear glaze. The rim of the lid and bottom of the box feet do not have to be glazed.

An optional step is to fire the piece again. When it cools, apply a mother-of-pearl luster over the simulated marble to give it an even more brilliant sheen.

▼ **10.** The finished jewel box is both a functional and decorative accessory for either a woman's dressing table or a man's bureau.

Glazing Techniques (Enamels or Varnishes): Decorating a Vase with Successive Glazes

Only a limited number of enamels can be mixed together. When you buy your paints, be sure to get a brochure giving specifications for the brand you choose.

Even though the steps for applying multiple glazes and the look they produce will vary depending on your brand and colors, the following general guidelines will be helpful.

Materials
- A red bisque vase or similar piece.
- Brushes: #4, 6 filberts.
- Paints: glazes—metallic, antique, gloss, and crystalline.

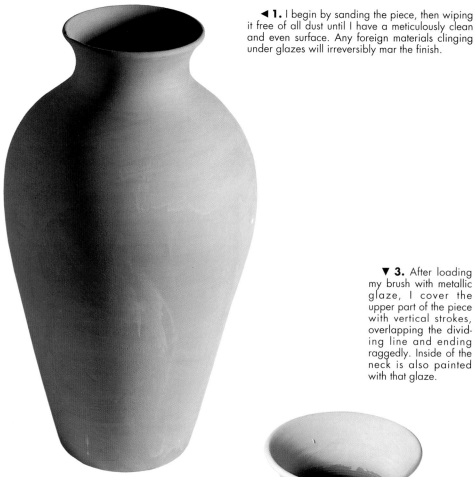

◄ **1.** I begin by sanding the piece, then wiping it free of all dust until I have a meticulously clean and even surface. Any foreign materials clinging under glazes will irreversibly mar the finish.

▼ **3.** After loading my brush with metallic glaze, I cover the upper part of the piece with vertical strokes, overlapping the dividing line and ending raggedly. Inside of the neck is also painted with that glaze.

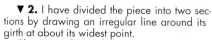

▼ **2.** I have divided the piece into two sections by drawing an irregular line around its girth at about its widest point.

Choosing glazes that are compatible, I'm also careful to select colors that all harmonize well with one another.

▶ **4**. Antique glaze is now applied to the bottom half, using vertical strokes, but this time worked from the bottom up, merging the two glazes at the dividing line. (A paper towel in the neck facilitates handling.)

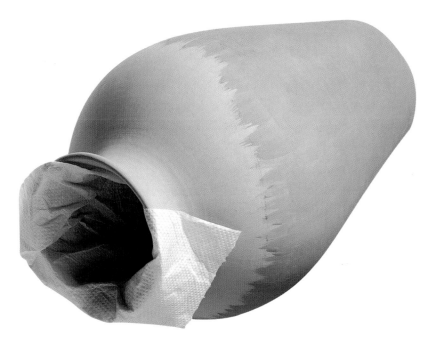

▼ **5.** Once the first coat is dry, I apply a gloss glaze over it, following the ragged pattern.

▲ **6.** Now I apply a second coat of metallic glaze to the top half, using brushwork in the same direction.

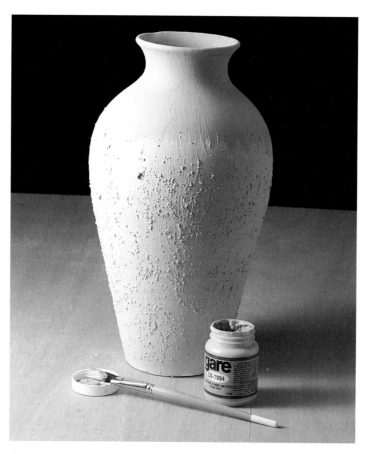

◀ **7.** When the previous coat on the lower half has dried, I repeat the procedure with a third coat, this time using crystalline glaze (note its texture), over which I will apply a second coat, once the first has dried.

▼ **8.** Now the final coat, a gloss glaze, goes over the lower half of the vase.

▼ **9.** Allowing each coat to dry before going to the next, I apply the last two coats of metallic glaze to the top half of the vase, then fire the piece.

▶ **10.** Successive layers of glaze produce fascinating and singular results with each project. Here, note the effective contrast between the one-tone metallic glaze on the upper part of the vase and the wonderfully variegated look produced by mixed glazes on the rest of the surface. Vertically applied brushstrokes also contribute to the success of this piece. I again stress the importance of directing your brushwork so that in divided pieces such as this example, the glazes of upper and lower portions flow the same way.

This was intended as a decorative vase, or perhaps to hold long reeds or other dry florals, so, as noted earlier, it was given interior glaze only on the inside of the neck, which is clearly visible. If the vase you decorate is meant to hold fresh flowers in water, then it's essential that the entire inner wall be coated with glaze.

Decorating a Spice Jar in the Majolica Technique

In the majolica technique, the object to be decorated is first coated with a white or light-colored satin-finish glaze; the design is then painted over the raw glaze with colored underglazes.

Using a thin, curling vine as my motif, I'll leave lots of white surface bare, a characteristic feature of majolica work. Such a design calls for delicate, flowing brushwork.

Materials

- A white bisque jar with lid.
- Brushes: #10 brights (for glazing), #2 and 4 rounds.
- Paints: medium blue, deep yellow, white satin glaze.
- Miscellaneous: palette, spatula, turpentine.

▲ **1.** A working sketch of a two-color vine pattern that flanks a diagonal band on which the word *thyme* (*tomillo* in Spanish) will be painted to identify the jar's intended contents.

◄ **2.** Following the usual steps, I prepare the piece for glazing by sanding and wiping down both the inside and outside walls.

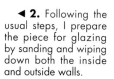

► **3.** It's wise to glaze any ceramic surface that comes into contact with food, so I apply two layers of satin glaze to the inside as well as to the outside of this spice holder; then I glaze the lid, allowing each surface to dry before going on to the next. Once it's dry, the jar is ready to receive its drawing.

▶ **4.** I wrap design transfer paper around the jar, place my sketch over it, then trace the design onto the jar's surface.

▶ **5.** This is how the piece looks once the drawing has been transferred.

◀ **6.** Using a #4 round brush dipped in yellow, I fill in each flower with a single stroke or two.

▶ **7.** With my #2 round brush dipped in blue, I paint the vine in a continuous stroke of uniform thinness, adjusting the traced drawing as I go along (pencil lines can be erased), and then paint each block letter in a single stroke.

▼ 8. Fine yellow and blue lines are now added diagonally and as accents around the jar's convex bands. The diagonal area for labeling is left blank here to help you lay out the lettering you might use.

▲► Alternative design. The sketch above and photograph below at right show a more complex design for an apothecary jar, also using the majolica technique. The pattern is inspired by a sixteenth-century Turkish beer jug.

Decorating an Urn with a Sponge Technique

Numerous decorative effects can easily be achieved with a sponge, depending on the texture of the sponge itself, the way it dabs on color, and how many colors are used.

Materials
- A white bisque pedestaled urn.
- Brush: #12 flat.
- Paint: white enamel, blue stroke (translucent underglaze) of two tones that blend easily.
- Tool: rough-grain sponge.

◀ **1.** As usual, sanding, burnishing, and, with a damp cloth, wiping the surface clean of all dust comes first. Next, white enamel for glazing the urn's interior is diluted in water. The liquid is poured into the jar and swigged around to bathe the entire inner wall. A wide brush is used to spread the glaze more evenly as needed, especially at the urn's neck. If your bisque is red clay, apply three coats of undiluted white enamel to the interior. However, if your urn has a narrow opening or you're sure the piece won't be used to hold liquid, skip the interior glazing.

◀ **2.** Using the #12 brush, I triple glaze the external surface, with drying time allowed between coats.

Not shown in this photo is my preparation of the two blue paints and application of the first over the white glaze. Since I've decided that my stroke colors are too concentrated for the subtle look I'm after, I dilute both blues with a few drops of water (whenever dilution is needed, be sure to use distilled water). When the blues are light enough—one a little paler than the other—I put the paler hue on the sponge and apply it with light touches, repeating the procedure as many times as needed to get good distribution over the whole surface. Now I wash the sponge, preparing it for the next step.

◄ 3. Once the first color has dried completely, I continue dabbing with the second blue, overlapping the two shades as I go, taking care not to cover the first totally. Note that lots of white ground is left exposed.

▼ 4. The second color has dried, producing a very subtle difference between the two blues, which was my aim with this finish. More contrast between tones of the same color is an equally attractive look. The piece is now ready for firing.

▼ 5. Close-up detail of the pattern produced by using a coarse-grained sponge.

Decorating a Saucer with the *Cuerda Seca* Technique

When adjacent glazes accidentally blend on a ceramic piece during firing, the chemical reaction can cause an undesirable effect. To prevent such an occurrence, colors can be separated with a line of underglaze. This simple method, known as *cuerda seca* (dry line), easily solves the problem, guaranteeing a clean firing every time.

Materials

- White bisque saucer (or coated with raw engobe, in which case, sanding is not required).
- Brushes: #4, 6, and 10 flats, #1 or 2 rounds.
- Paints: strokes (translucent underglaze) in very dark brown or black; opaque glazes (antique or art glaze) in light green, dark green, and red; art glaze in light tan (or other pale neutral).

◄ **1.** Using colored pencils, I draw a design that is simple but bold enough to fill up most of the surface to be decorated.

► **2.** As always, I begin by sanding and cleaning the surface. I've chosen a saucer rather than a plate for this project to demonstrate that in contemporary patterns, the indentation for a cup is often ignored in laying out the design, whereas traditional patterns usually concentrate saucer motifs around the rim, leaving the center unadorned.

◄ 3. Using pencil, I've made a freehand copy of my design on the saucer.

▼ 4. With a #1 round brush I outline the drawing with a uniform line; the #2 brush is used for the thicker twig. (Whenever this technique is used, plan good color harmony between the outline and fill-in colors.)

Starting with the lighter green, I begin painting in my glazes. Three coats of it, with drying time between, will be applied before I go to the next color. A #4 or 6 flat brush or #2 round are equally suitable here. I take care not to touch the brown outline with underglaze.

◀ **5.** For the pale tan background tone, I begin by painting around the drawing in a flowing brushstroke, taking great care not to overlap the cuerda seca—the brown underglaze lines.

▶ **6.** Once I have gone around the design (and filled in all little spaces between the cherries and twigs), I glaze the entire surface. Repeating the procedure two more times, I let each coat dry before applying the next. The saucer is now ready to be fired.

Decorating a Box with a Reserve Technique

Using liquid latex, you can mask areas of your design that you wish to remain free of color. This enables you to work slowly and without fear of staining the piece. Another advantage of latex is that you can easily peel it off after it has served its purpose.

Materials
- A white bisque box.
- Brushes: #12 flat, #1, 2, and 4 rounds.
- Paint: lavender opaque glaze (or underglazed engobe); clear overglaze.
- Liquid latex.

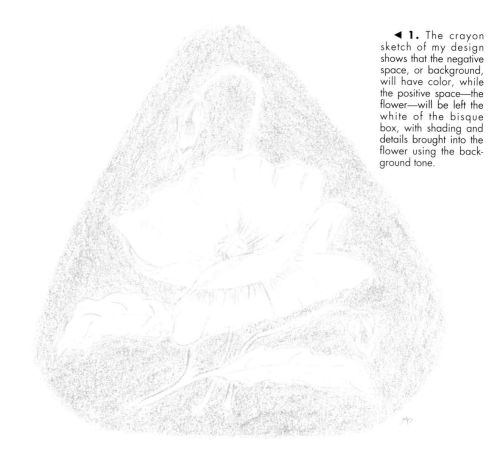

◀ **1.** The crayon sketch of my design shows that the negative space, or background, will have color, while the positive space—the flower—will be left the white of the bisque box, with shading and details brought into the flower using the background tone.

◀ 2. I begin by cleaning and burnishing the base and lid with sandpaper to prepare it for decorating.

▶ **3.** The box is now ready to be decorated. I've decided that the inside of both the base and lid will be left white. If they were to be painted lavender or a complementary color, those interior glazes would be the first applied when I get to that step.

▼ **4.** Drawing the design on the box, I silhouette it only. All shading and details of line work in the petals, buds, and leaves will be painted freehand later.

▲ 5. First I wet my brush, dip it in latex, and give a broad outline to the large flower. Then I fill in all smaller elements of the drawing: buds, stems, and leaves. By protecting, or reserving, those areas with latex, I ensure that they will remain white, since colored glaze cannot get to them.

◄ 6. With a #12 flat brush, I spread underglaze over the entire outer surface of both the base and lid. The #4 round brush is used for tight spaces—between the stems, for example. If the brush happens to hit the latex, it won't matter, but I must take care not to stain the drawing's unprotected central area. Three layers should be applied, with usual drying time between coats.

◄ **7.** Using a pointed instrument, I lift a corner of the latex, then peel it off entirely. (An ordinary tweezer is an efficient tool for this job.)

► **8.** With the latex completely and cleanly removed, a careful inspection should be made to see that no little remnants remain.

◄ 9. Now all the detail work is applied with a careful and precise hand. Using #1 and 2 round brushes dipped in the lavender underglaze applied as background color, I refer to my original sketch and paint in all the shading and fine lines—some a bit thicker than others where deeper shadows so indicate.

◄ 10. After the underglaze has dried thoroughly, I apply two coats of transparent glaze, with drying time between them. After firing, the finished box is ready to be displayed or wrapped up for gift giving.

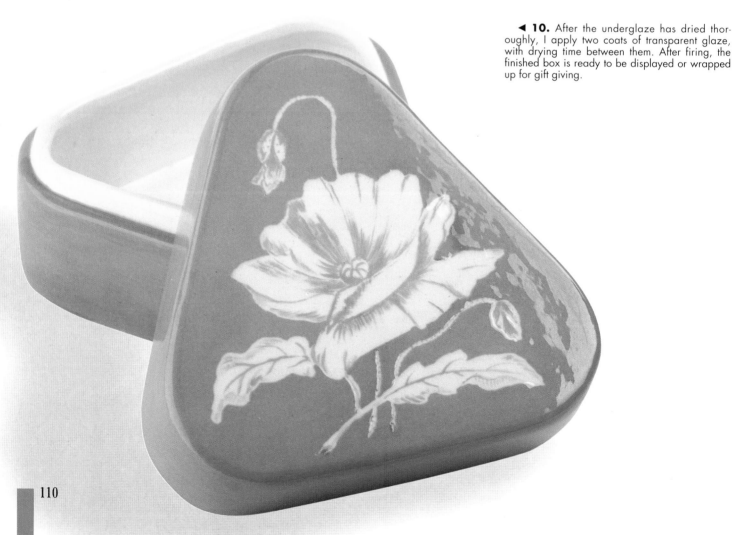

Overglaze Technique: Questions to Consider Before Painting on Porcelain

Before painting on porcelain, clean the surface with a cloth soaked in denatured alcohol. The drawing can be transferred or drawn with pencil directly on the piece. The whole background doesn't have to be white; you can work on clear glaze that has been fired beforehand or even color part of the background, reserving a white area for the drawing.

If latex is applied as a mask, color is spread by sponge, the latex is peeled off, and the piece is fired. The same look can be achieved without latex by painting the design first, then firing it to fix the colors—which makes it easier to lay down background tone next. If some stains are produced through firing, they can easily be cleaned off with a cotton swab soaked in denatured alcohol.

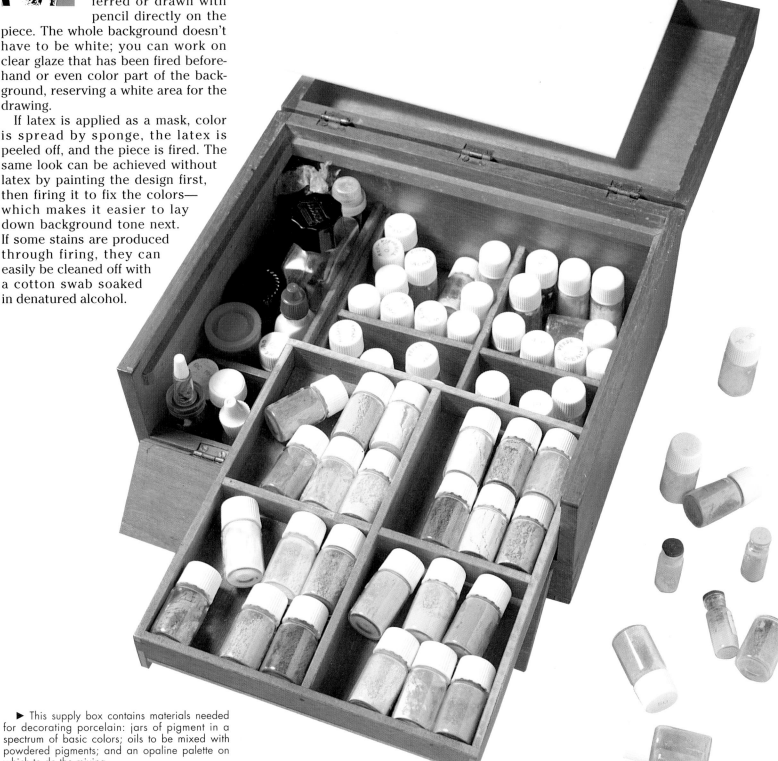

▶ This supply box contains materials needed for decorating porcelain: jars of pigment in a spectrum of basic colors; oils to be mixed with powdered pigments; and an opaline palette on which to do the mixing.

A porcelain background tone should be completely even. Since brushes often leave visible brushstrokes, it's better to apply background color with a fine sponge soaked in diluted pigment, working in small, light dabs.

Porcelain glaze absorbs very little color, so to achieve the desired shade—anywhere from light to very dark—successive layers must be applied, with firings in between. But another option is available. In addition to this traditional method, today, commercial paints are sold ready to use, thus bypassing multiple firings.

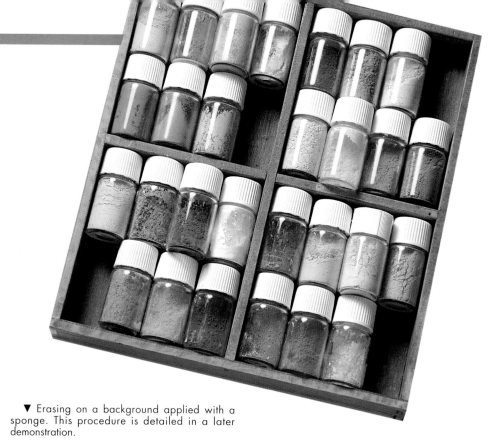

▼ Erasing on a background applied with a sponge. This procedure is detailed in a later demonstration.

Decorating a Porcelain Plate with Daisies

In this overglaze technique, decoration is applied to the surface of a porcelain piece that has been glazed and fired beforehand. The pigments chosen have been mixed with oil to form a creamy paste.

The brushstrokes are loose and light, lending a delicate, transparent air to the design.

Materials
- Porcelain plate.
- Brushes: #2, 4, and 6 flats; #2 and 4 brights.
- Pigments: light yellow, dark yellow, brown, light green, dark green, medium blue, violet.
- Solvent: lavender oil (to mix with pigments).
- Palette: opaline glass or glazed white tile.
- Tool: spatula, medium size with rounded end.
- Miscellaneous: denatured alcohol, turpentine.

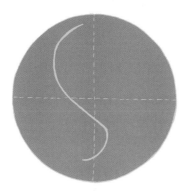

◀ **1.** Preparing my plate design (which I happen to draw on red paper with a yellow pencil), I divide my pattern in quadrants to help direct the layout.

▲ **2.** The design flows in a graceful S curve.

▶ **3.** The daisies, as shown in this final drawing, will not be painted white on the plate; rather, the white of the porcelain, delineated by surrounding colors, will define the daisies.

◀ **4.** I begin by cleaning the plate, then wiping it with a rag soaked in alcohol. The colors are prepared on an opaline palette (or an ordinary glazed white wall tile) by mixing a small amount of pigment powder and a few drops of oil with a spatula until it acquires a soft, pastelike consistency. I usually prepare the colors one by one on a tile, then place them all on the larger surface of my palette.

◄ **5.** Repeating the procedure used for my preliminary sketch, I divide the plate into four equal parts, deciding how I want to orient the design so that if the plate hangs on a wall, a mark can be made on the back at top center for a hook attachment.

► **6.** Daisies are easy flowers to draw and always look fresh and appealing on porcelain. The largest cluster is drawn at the top of the S curve, the main focal point. Then I add some buds and leaves along the rest of the curve.

▲ **7.** This is a preview of the plate as it will look almost completely decorated. You can see that although the leaves are important, they really serve as background for the daisies and to balance gaps here and there, so some of them are left unfinished or deliberately faint.

▲ **8.** The center of attraction is wherever the viewer's eye is drawn first. As shown in close-up, in this design our focus is directed to the daisy threesome, which employs the important design principle that an odd, rather than even, number of like motifs makes a more interesting and animated composition. The triangular arrangement I've used is also a tried-and-true basic design layout.

Beginning with the central daisies, I paint their pale yellow centers with a #6 flat brush, filling each oval shape lightly so that paint doesn't build up at the edges. The uneven border is painted with dark yellow, then partially highlighted in brown, using a #2 or 4 flat brush.

◄ **9.** Although I leave the daisy petals white, I enliven them by adding a few shadows, using #2 and 4 bright brushes. My colors are subtle touches of brown, yellow, violet, and blue applied in short brushstrokes toward the flowers' centers. Note that shading is kept on the same side of each flower center to establish the direction from which light shines on the grouping, creating a more realistic, dimensional look. I use very pale violet and blue shadows on the petals in the same fashion, then put a highlight on the lighter areas by going over them with a dry brush.

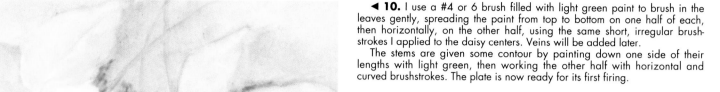

◄ **10.** I use a #4 or 6 brush filled with light green paint to brush in the leaves gently, spreading the paint from top to bottom on one half of each, then horizontally, on the other half, using the same short, irregular brushstrokes I applied to the daisy centers. Veins will be added later.

The stems are given some contour by painting down one side of their lengths with light green, then working the other half with horizontal and curved brushstrokes. The plate is now ready for its first firing.

▲ **11.** Removed from the kiln, the plate is sanded down, then cleaned with a cloth soaked in denatured alcohol to prepare it for the final steps: completing the shading and details.

Even though the white daisies stand out against their green leaves, you might want to add a background color: a natural hue such as sky blue, sunshine yellow, grass green, pale sand or earth. This tint can be included before the first firing, but if you are still relatively inexperienced, it is advisable to fix the painting first. Then, if you don't like the background you have applied, it can be wiped off without endangering your detailed work on the pattern. Long strokes should be applied as background tone, working from the edge to the center. The tone can actually be gradually lightened so that the plate's rim has the faintest layer of paint.

◄ **12.** Some further touching up is now done on outlining and shading the flowers.

► **13.** More sheen and color are applied to the leaves to suggest highlights and to deepen shadows. When these details produce the delicate light-and-shadow effect this porcelain piece should have, you may consider the work finished after the second firing, and skip a third firing.

After the second firing, I gently sand down the plate and clean it with denatured alcohol. Brushes are cleaned with turpentine.

▼ **14.** I now consider the decoration to be finished, although another crowning accent could be added: a rim of gold around the outside lip, in which case, the plate would have to be fired one more time.

Decorating a Tray with the Paint/Remove Method

The technique in this demonstration is quite simple and fun to do: putting paint down and then removing it.

The process gradually accentuates shadows and highlights, building contour and volume into a design. Once again overglaze pigments are used, but this exercise gives you an opportunity to try another method of decorating with them.

Materials

- Porcelain plate or tray.
- Brushes: #4 or 6 flats (for background); #1 and 2 rounds (for details).
- Pigment: dark green (any dark pigment will do).
- Solvent: lavender oil (to mix with pigments).
- Palette: opaline glass or glazed tile.
- Tool: spatula, medium size with rounded end.
- Other colorant (optional): India ink.
- Miscellaneous: denatured alcohol, turpentine.

▲ **1.** The plate is cleaned with a cloth soaked in denatured alcohol, an important step in this process, as all natural oils from hands touching the plate must be removed.

◄ **2.** I either draw directly or, in this case, trace down my pattern using design transfer paper.

▲ **3.** To emphasize the pattern, I take the optional step of going over it with India ink, making sure it dries before applying paint.

▶ **4.** With the green overglaze mixture (pigment plus oil) I've prepared, I coat the surface of the plate, using broad, soft strokes. This procedure may also be performed with a sponge instead of a brush.

Another solution I've readied ahead of time is a blend, in equal parts, of lavender oil and alcohol. With a #6 brush cleaned in turpentine, I dip into the solution, wipe excess off on a cloth (so it won't drip), then start removing glaze from the large leaf first.

◄ 5. Now I remove glaze from the grapes, using a #4 brush dipped in the solution, working with circular brushstrokes to follow the contours of the fruit.

By erasing more lightly, a shadow effect is created; by pressing down more firmly, shiny highlights come into the picture.

Whenever the brush picks up too much glaze in this removal process, I wash it in turpentine, then continue erasing until the whole drawing has been gone over.

▼ 6. A #6 flat brush lends an interesting texture to the negative space—the background green. With the brush held in an almost vertical position, I add several delicate accents to positive spaces within the design.

This technique can be adapted to multiple colors within one decoration, combining various tones in both your background and/or design motif. Experiment by going as far as your imagination takes you.

Decorating a Box with a Water-and-Sugar Technique

This technique is quite similar to *cuerda seca*. The mix of pigment with water and sugar produces an extremely fast-drying paint. A very fine line applied with a nib prevents the paint colors from mixing together.

Materials

- Porcelain box with lid.
- Brushes: #2 and 4 flats.
- Pigments: red, yellow, blue, purple, green.
- Solvent: lavender oil (to mix with pigments).
- Palette: opaline glass or glazed tile.
- Tool: spatula, medium size with rounded end.
- Other colorant: India ink.
- Solvent: distilled water and powdered sugar.
- Tool: pen nib for India ink.
- Miscellaneous: denatured alcohol, turpentine.

▲ **1.** Based on typical chinoiserie motifs, this drawing is a particularly appropriate choice for a traditional lidded box.

◄ **2.** As always, porcelain must be cleaned thoroughly with alcohol to prepare it for decorating.

121

◄ **3.** Note that when the drawing is transferred to the box lid, lots of open white space remains, as is very characteristic of Chinese-inspired porcelain pieces.

► **4.** I place equal parts of black pigment and sugar on my palette and prepare to dilute the mixture with distilled water.

▶ **5.** Using a round-tipped spatula and adding more distilled water as needed, I mix the blend thoroughly until it has the fluid consistency of ink.

▶ **6.** I dip a pen nib in this mixture and outline my drawing. The line dries very quickly, enabling me to begin adding color immediately, having earlier prepared all of my pigment-and-oil glazes. The black outlines will not run or spread when in contact with the glazes.

► **7.** With all the colors now in place, note that some are applied more loosely than others, as on the clouds and parts of the birds, simulating the effect of watercolor painting.

◄ **8.** For the base of the box, I had prepared a larger amount of red, which I've brushed on (a sponge may be used instead). I've taken advantage of a design feature built into the base—the molded grooves left unglazed to form an attractive stripe accent.

▶ **9.** The lid is now ready for the kiln; the base will also be fired. Note that this overglaze technique requires a single firing only.

▶ **10.** Studying this close-up detail, you can appreciate the tonal variations produced by different underglazes and varying brushwork.

▼ **11.** The base and lid have now been fired. Any of the colors in the lid design might have been selected as a coordinate for the base, but soft red seemed the best choice to balance the few accents of that color near the top of the lid.

Decorating a Pitcher with a Dusting Technique

T he dusting technique is for darkening only parts of a piece to create a very strong contrast with lighter areas. Since this is a rather laborious process, confining it to just one section of a piece is recommended, which is how it will be demonstrated in our example.

Dusting is generally used for backgrounds or restricted to accent areas of a given color, although several colors may be included. The technique can be applied only after areas not destined to be dusted have been fired.

Materials
- Small porcelain pitcher.
- Brushes: #2, 4, 6 rounds; #10 flat.
- Pigments: blue, green, brown, pink.
- Solvents: mineral oil for pigments; copaiba oil for dusting.
- Palette: opaline glass or glazed tile.
- Tool: spatula, medium size with rounded end.
- Miscellaneous: denatured alcohol, cloth pad, absorbent cotton.

► **1.** Both sides of my pitcher design are shown in these sketches; the dusted areas, penciled light blue here, will be painted very dark blue. Pitchers and bowls present more challenging design options than the flat surfaces of plates and trays. As shown here, a pattern may flow as connected art from one side to the other, but with different layouts on each contour. Another approach is to repeat the motif at regular intervals on all sides.

◄ **2.** As with all porcelain pieces, the surface of this pitcher must be cleaned thoroughly with denatured alcohol before it may be decorated.

127

▶ **3.** Having mixed my pigments with oil and readied them on my palette, I transfer my drawing to the pitcher. Note that the top of the drawing—the flowers, leaves, and vines—all connect, forming a continuous border or holding line against which the dark-blue dusting will abut.

▼ **4.** I begin my brushwork by applying pink to the blossoms and green to the leaves and stems, using #4 and 6 brushes. Then I fire the piece.

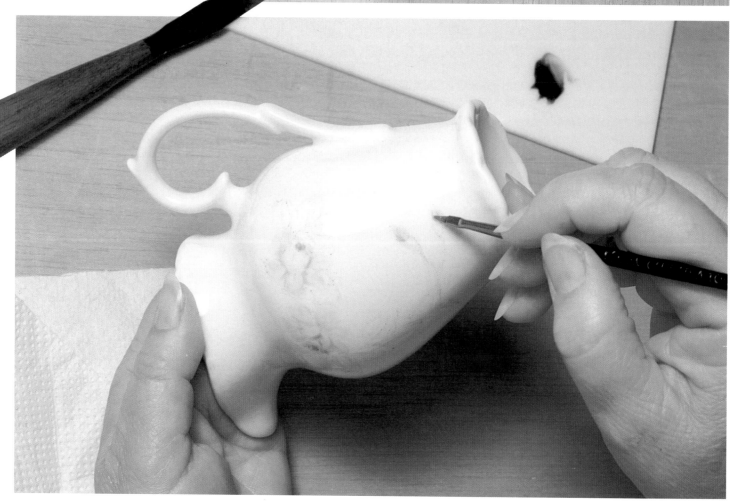

▶ **5.** With a #2 brush used for accent details, I go over the pink, intensifying it here and there to suggest shadow and contour, then I shade the stems with brown and give the pitcher its second firing.

◀ **6.** This close-up detail of the previous step shows subtle gradations in the greens and pinks—important differences that impart realistic light-and-shadow effects.

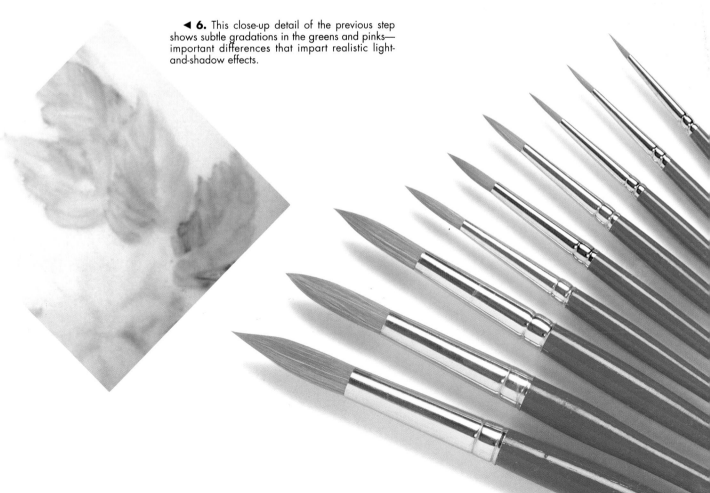

▶ **7.** The dusting technique is employed after the second firing. Referring to my original sketch, I coat those parts of the pitcher that are to be blue with copaiba oil, using a cloth pad (or brush) to spread the oil evenly and making sure that none of it touches the drawing. I will let the oil set for a day before proceeding.

▼ **8.** I place some powered blue pigment on my palette, smoothing out any lumps. Then I pick up some pigment with a wad of cotton and drop it on the oiled surface using very gentle dabs. I make sure the wad is loaded with enough pigment so that mainly the pigment and not the cotton touches the oiled surface. This procedure should be repeated several times to get as much powder as possible on all the designated areas. If it is absolutely necessary, you can remove some of the pigment very carefully, using a soft brush.

When I finish applying the powdered pigment, the piece is ready for firing. Once the pigment powder has been absorbed by the oil, the piece cannot be dusted a second time, although after firing it, you may repeat the entire process to intensify the color.

► **9.** This close-up detail shows the texture and intensity of an area dusted with blue pigment. The depth of its color will contrast richly with the light floral design.

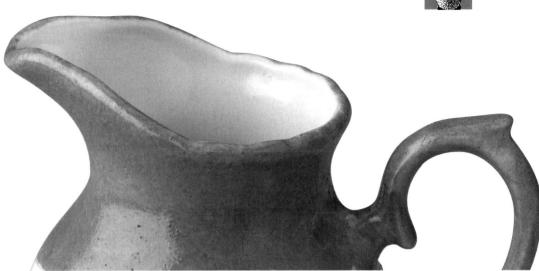

▼ **10.** When the dusting process is concluded, any excess pigment can be saved on a piece of paper, folded and kept for future use. Don't return excess pigment to its original bottle, since it's almost certain to contain tiny strands of cotton.

▶ **11.** In this close-up detail of the finished work the grainy texture of the dusted background may be seen. Also note a clear demarcation between the pale roses and pale leaves, achieved by subtly accenting the pink with deeper pink at the petals' edges. Those details should be checked along the way and rectified as needed between firings.

◀ **12.** A dramatic contrast between the textured dark blue and the smooth, pale floral gives this pitcher its distinctive appeal. I hope you'll agree that the painstaking dusting technique is well worth the time and effort it requires.

Decorating a Plate with the Hua-Kao Technique

If you have tried these exercises in sequence, by now, as we begin our final demonstration, you're familiar enough with some procedures that apply to various techniques to be working with more ease and confidence.

In fact, this final technique is similar to an earlier one: the paint/remove method used on a tray. But with the Hua-Kao technique, more colors are employed. We will remove and add paint with delicate but definite brush-strokes for a soft, diffused look.

Materials
- Porcelain plate.
- Brushes: #4 and 12 flats; #0 and 1 rounds; fan blender; eraser brush.
- Pigments: purple, lavender, pink, brown, light green, yellow, light blue, red.
- Solvent: lavender oil (to mix with pigments).
- Tools: spatula (medium-size) with rounded end; dabber with handle; eraser.
- Palette: opaline glass or glazed tile.
- Miscellaneous: denatured alcohol, turpentine.

◄ **1.** My colored drawing suggests the diffused look that is characteristic of the Hua-Kao technique to be used.

► **2.** My first step, as always, is to clean the porcelain with alcohol. Then the design will be transferred to the plate.

133

◄ **4.** My background tone, which goes over the whole drawing, will have areas of yellow, lavender, and green, with lavender dominating. (You may have to darken your pencil drawing to keep it visible; my pencil drawing is too faint to be seen in this photograph.) I start by painting several delicate strokes with a #12 brush for each color, mixing them where they merge. A cloth dabber is also useful for blending.

▼ **3.** I blend the pigments with oil and place them on an opaline palette. Note how little of each color is required; a little bit goes a long way.

▼ **5.** With the #12 brush, I have added purple to intensify lavender in the area designated for the flowers. There must be no accumulation of glaze; it should be kept thin and flowing.

I define the flowers and leaves now by erasing them with the same brush. Then to soften them, I use a fan brush.

▶ **6.** Now using both the eraser and its brush end, I finish removing paint and start shaping the floral petals.

◀ **7.** With a #4 flat brush dipped in green, I apply that base color to the leaves.

After cleaning the brush, I paint the flowers sparingly with blue, purple, and pink. The leaves and background are also painted, some areas deeper than others. Details within the flowers are worked with fine #0 and 1 round brushes; brown is added to stems.

I clean my brushes frequently during this work, first dipping them in alcohol, then in oil, then wiping them dry with a paper towel, being careful to keep the bristles straight. (Even when you're not changing colors, a brush should be oiled now and again, but remember to remove excess oil.)

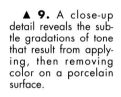

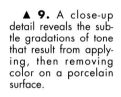

▲ **9.** A close-up detail reveals the subtle gradations of tone that result from applying, then removing color on a porcelain surface.

▼ **8.** The many diffused colors worked ever so subtly over the surface of the porcelain give it a luminous quality that is hard to match using any other technique.

It should be pointed out, however, that although this method requires only one firing, beginners may need to do several before achieving just the right effect. First attempts can be rectified through additional firings until the desired look emerges.

With the Hua-Kao technique, variations are always possible, as they are with all the porcelain decoration methods reviewed earlier—and all the demonstrations for other classifications of ceramics adornment that preceded those. Here, as throughout the book, the steps presented are meant to get you going. As you continue to grow in this craft, you'll probably even want to combine and devise various other techniques on your own.

GLOSSARY

A

Arita. Japanese place of origin of Imari porcelain ware created in the seventeenth century for export to European cities.

B

Banding wheel. A device consisting of a platform mounted on a shaft for modeling clay and for decorating it. Found in different shapes and sizes and driven by hand, foot, or electrically.

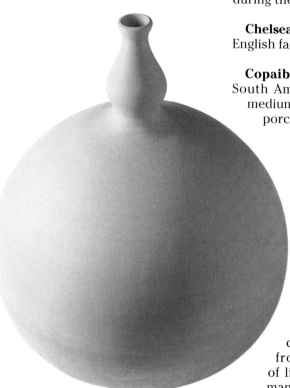

Bisque. (Also called biscuit.) Ware subjected to a first firing, hard yet still porous.

Bisque-firing. First firing of raw clay to harden a piece prior to glazing.

Böttger. Material named for the discoverer of the first porcelain formula in Europe.

C

Ceramics. Clay objects that have undergone a chemical transformation during the firing process.

Chelsea. Porcelain produced by an English factory since 1745.

Copaiba oil. Oil extracted from a South American tree and used as a medium for preparing overglazes in porcelain decoration.

Crackling. Almost invisible cracks produced by a sudden cooling of the glaze or differing rates of contraction for the clay and the glaze. They can be deliberately obtained to produce a particular effect.

Cuerda seca. (Spanish for "dry line.") Method of decorating pottery in which glazes of different colors are kept separate from one another by means of lines drawn in a mixture of manganese and grease.

D

Decal. A design on special paper with metallic oxide colors and oil base. Decals are stuck to ceramic before firing and then burned off, transferring the design to the piece.

Decoration. Elements or motifs used to decorate a piece. There are three basic kinds: applied, incised, painted.

Deflocculent. A substance that liquefies a material in a solvent, usually water, such as soluble glass.

Delft. Tin-glazed earthenware of Dutch origin. Often also used to refer to English porcelain.

Denatured alcohol. Used to clean porcelain objects before painting on them; also for cleaning brushes used to apply gold, platinum, and lusters. With other substances, part of a mixture for certain decorating techniques.

E

Engobe. French word for slip, and often used interchangeably with that term, engobe is clay mixed with water to a fluid, creamy consistency, used for decorating.

F

Faïence. French name for the city of Faenza, Italy, a major producer of porous ceramics covered with lead or tin glazes.

Feldspar. A mineral belonging to the aluminum silicate group, one of the main ingredients of glazes and porcelains.

Fire. The action of firing a piece in the kiln.

Firing atmosphere. Formed by the gases inside the kiln during the firing process.

Flux. Substance added to glazes and clays to promote melting and glazing.

Flux point. Temperature at which the glaze melts.

Frit. Glass that has been melted and ground into a powder, added to clay and glazes to promote vitrification.

G

Glaze. Vitreous layer covering an object to be fired. It seals the pores and improves the finish. Can be transparent, opaque, matte, glossy, colored, or colorless, depending on its composition.

Glazing. Action of covering a raw or bisque-fired piece with glaze by dipping, pouring, spraying, or brushing on. Different glazes can be used on the same piece to achieve special effects.

Grog. Fired and ground clay added to the clay body to increase porosity and reduce contraction during drying and firing.

H

High-temperature colors. Colors fired at the same time as the glaze.

Hizen. Japanese province where the specific combination of minerals was found for the manufacture of porcelain.

I

Imari. Richly decorated porcelain made in seventeenth-century Japan for export markets, named for its port of origin.

K

Kakiemon. Fine-quality Japanese porcelain sparsely decorated with overglaze enamels, a style that spread throughout China and Europe.

Kaolin. Word derived from *kao-ling,* which in Chinese means high hill, the place where the mineral used for porcelain was found; a fine white clay used in ceramics, especially for making porcelain.

L

Leatherhard. Term applied to clay that has dried but still retains enough plasticity for cutting if not for molding.

Luster. Decorative finish that has a metallic, lustrous appearance.

M

Majolica. Name derived from Majorca, an island port midway between the Italian and Iberian peninsulas. First used for Spanish-Moorish ceramics with luster, although it later came to designate any ceramics with a tin glaze.

Medici. Artificial porcelain with symmetrical, floral designs in white and blue.

Meissen. Type of German porcelain that copied Japanese designs but later developed its own style.

Monochrome. Decoration using a single color.

O

Overglazes. Also called low-temperature glazes, they are applied over fired glazes or enamels.

Oxidation. A chemical process that takes place during firing, when the atmosphere of the kiln is highly oxygenated.

▶ **PYROMETRIC CONES**

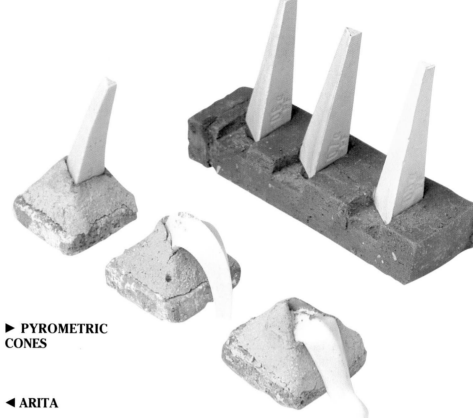

◀ **ARITA**

◀ **SLIP**

◀ **RAKU**

▼ **BISQUE**

▶ **IMARI**

▲ FAÏENCE

▲ TERRA-COTTA

▲ MAJOLICA

◄ KAKIEMON

▲ LUSTER

▼ GROG

◄ ► PORCELAIN

141

P

Plasticity. A characteristic of clay that can be molded and permanently retain its shape.

Porcelain. Ceramic product based on a mixture of kaolin, feldspar, and quartz as its raw materials. China was the birthplace of porcelain, which is why the word *china* is also used in English to describe porcelain.

Pyrometric cones. Elongated three-sided pyramids (about two inches tall) made of various combinations of ceramic materials formulated to soften and bend when subjected to specific kiln heat, thereby indicating firing temperatures to be used.

Q

Quartz. A mineral consisting of silicon dioxide, an essential ingredient for making porcelain.

R

Raku. Meaning *happiness* in Japanese, a term used to describe ceramics created for tea services, usually of irregular shape and texture.

Reducing. A chemical process taking place during firing, when the atmosphere of the kiln lacks oxygen.

Running. Unpredictable shapes produced when using a glaze with a low flux point that melts during firing.

S

Sgraffito. Italian word for scratched, a technique whereby engobe is scratched with a pointed instrument to reveal underlying color.

Sèvres. A French porcelain characterized by its heavy decoration, abundant use of gold, and beautiful background colors.

Shrinkage. A reduction in size of a piece that takes place during drying or firing, due to water evaporation and other chemical processes.

Slip. Watery clay mixture used for decorating and for joining pieces together, as in attaching handles to pots.

Staffordshire. A salt glaze ceramic inferior in quality and beauty to true porcelain.

T

Terra-cotta. From the Italian meaning baked earth, applied to dark, fired clay that is unglazed and therefore porous.

Turpentine. An oily substance extracted from certain trees, mainly conifers, and used as a solvent in porcelain painting.

U

Underglazes. Colors applied directly to bisque, then covered with transparent glaze.

V

Viscosity. A property of fluids that diminishes slippage. A glaze is viscous, as it does not run after being applied.

Vitrification. A physical and chemical process taking place at high temperature, causing glaze on the surface of a piece to form an even, nonporous layer.

W

White mineral oil. Derived from petroleum after refining and decoloring. Used for preparing powdered paint for porcelain decoration (china paints).

Worcester. An English porcelain, combining drawings of both European and Chinese style. Successfully used for relief molding.

Acknowledgments

Parramón Ediciones expresses gratitude to all those who participated in the Spanish edition of this book.

First and foremost, to **M. Pilar Navarro**, who wrote all the text, devised the demonstrations, and provided many illustrative drawings. She was not only open to suggestions made throughout the editing process, but also gave indispensable general guidance about ceramics decoration gleaned from her many years of experience in the field.

Josep Guasch was in charge of the overall design of the book and page-by-page layouts. The result speaks for itself, clearly showing the comprehensive effort and talent that went into producing this volume.

Developing a book of this complexity demands a constant eagle eye on myriad details requiring ongoing tracking and correction. This difficult and often thankless job fell to the very able **Jordi Martínez**, to whom sincere thanks are extended.

Our gratitude also goes to Jordi Segú for furnishing several drawings; to Manuel Vilasaló for his contribution to production meetings and overall assistance; and to Montserrat Roura, M. Paz Vilasaló, Sofía Ciro, and Group IV of the School of Fine Arts for the loan of several of their works as illustrations for this book. We also acknowledge with thanks all the museums, institutions, and private individuals who made material and information available for this project. Sincere thanks, too, to all who participated in the technical aspects of this book at all stages of its production.

Jordi Vigué
Editorial Director